THE CHINESE MIND

Other Books by the Author

Asian Face Reading
Business Guide to Japan
Chinese Etiquette & Ethics in Business
Chinese in Plain English
Etiquette Guide to Japan
Instant Japanese
Japanese Business Dictionary
Japanese Etiquette & Ethics in Business
Japanese in Plain English
Japan Made Easy
Japan's Cultural Code Words
KATA: The Key to Understanding & Dealing with the Japanese
Korea's Business & Cultural Code Words
Korean Business Etiquette
Korean in Plain English
Tokyo Transit Guide
Survival Japanese
The Chinese Have a Word for It
The Japanese Have a Word for It
The Japanese Samurai Code
Japan Unmasked
Samurai Strategies
Sex and the Japanese
Instant Korean
Survival Korean
Instant Chinese
Survival Chinese
Dining Guide to Japan
Shopping Guide to Japan
Etiquette Guide to China
Etiquette Guide to Korea

THE CHINESE MIND

BOYÉ LAFAYETTE DE MENTE

UNDERSTANDING TRADITIONAL CHINESE BELIEFS AND
THEIR INFLUENCE ON CONTEMPORARY CULTURE

TUTTLE PUBLISHING
Tokyo • Rutland, Vermont • Singapore

Published by Tuttle Publishing, an imprint of Periplus Editions (HK) Ltd., with editorial offices at 364 Innovation Drive, North Clarendon, Vermont 05759 U.S.A.

Library of Congress Cataloging-in-Publication Data

De Mente, Boye.
  The Chinese mind : understanding traditional Chinese beliefs and their influence on contemporary culture / Boye Lafayette De Mente. -- 1st ed.
      p. cm.
  ISBN 978-0-8048-4011-8 (pbk.)
1. China--Civilization. 2. Chinese language--Terms and phrases. I. Title. II. Title:
Understanding traditional Chinese beliefs and their influence on contemporary culture.
  DS721.D386 2009
  306.0951--dc22
                          2008043182

ISBN 978-0-8048-4011-8

Distributed by

North America, Latin America & Europe
Tuttle Publishing
364 Innovation Drive,
North Clarendon, VT 05759-9436 U.S.A.
Tel: 1 (802) 773-8930
Fax: 1 (802) 773-6993
info@tuttlepublishing.com
www.tuttlepublishing.com

Asia Pacific
Berkeley Books Pte. Ltd.
61 Tai Seng Avenue #02-12
Singapore 534167
Tel: (65) 6280-1330
Fax: (65) 6280-6290
inquiries@periplus.com.sg
www.periplus.com

Japan
Tuttle Publishing
Yaekari Building, 3rd Floor
5-4-12 Osaki, Shinagawa-ku
Tokyo 141 0032
Tel: (81) 3 5437-0171; Fax: (81) 3 5437-0755
tuttle-sales@gol.com
www.periplus.com

First edition
13 12 11 10 09   6 5 4 3 2 1

Printed in United States

TUTTLE PUBLISHING® is a registered trademark of Tuttle Publishing,
a division of Periplus Editions (HK) Ltd.

CONTENTS

NOTES ON CHINA

The Name of China in Chinese

The proper name of China in Mandarin Chinese is *Zhong Guo* (Johhng Gwah), usually written in Roman letters as one word: Zhongguo. Zhong means "central" or "middle" and guo means "kingdom"—thus the English language references to China as the "Central Kingdom" or "Middle Kingdom." This is the name that was adopted in medieval times when the Chinese considered themselves the most advanced people on earth (rightly so in many ways) and looked upon people on their borders and elsewhere as barbarians.

Origin of the Name China

The origin of the name "China" is not clear, but there are several stories. Marco Polo, the famed Italian adventurer who spent several years in China (1275-1292 A.D.) called the country "Chin"—apparently a reference to the Chin or *Qin* (Cheen) empire of the 3rd century B.C. "Shina" (She-nah) was another ancient reference to at least a part of the huge area now known as China.

It seems that two early Portuguese visitors to the country—Barbosa in 1516 and Garcia de Orta in 1563—may have been the first ones to refer to the country as "China" in their writing about the "Middle Kingdom."

The official English name of the country is the People's Republic of China (PRC).

The Ethnic Makeup of China

Some 90 percent of the one billion-plus population of China is made up of so-called "Han Chinese"—that is, Chinese who racially and ethnically trace their ancestry back to the Han clan, founders of the great Han Dynasty (206 B.C.–220 A.D.), considered one of the greatest periods in the history of China. This was the period when Confucianism became the official doctrine of the government, and when amazing advances were made in agriculture and various scientific and technological fields.

During and following the Han Dynasty many other clans, including the Yi, Qian, Di, and Man, became integrated into the Han people. Today Han Chinese are found in all parts of the country, but mainly in the middle and lower reaches of the Yellow River, Yangtze River, Pearl River, and the Northeast Plain—which encompass most of central and eastern China.

There are 53 minority ethnic groups in China with their own languages, and 23 that have their own systems of writing. Most of these groups live in the vast border regions of the west, southwest, and northwest. The ancestral homeland of the Zhuang, the largest of the minority groups (with a population in excess of 12 million) takes up much of the southwestern region of the country.

Many visitors to Xinkiang in the far west are surprised to discover that the Uighar people of the province are Muslims, and that their culture is Central Asian rather than Chinese.

The Administrative Makeup of China

China is the third largest nation in the world (after Russia and Canada), with over 1.3 billion people. It is made up of 23 provinces, five huge so-called autonomous regions (Guangxi, Inner Mongolia, Ningxia, Tibet/Xizang and Xinjiang), and four municipalities (Beijing, Chungqing, Shanghai and Tianjin). The four municipalities have the same kind of governments as the provinces, and each has a population in excess of ten million. Hong Kong and Macau are self-governing Special Administrative Regions (SARs).

The Chinese Language

There are seven, eight, or ten different languages in China (depending on who is counting) and several dozen dialects. The main language groups are *Putonghua* (Mandarian), *Yue* (Cantonese), *Wu* (Shanghaiese), *Gan*, *Kejia* (Hakka), *Min* (Fuzhou) and *Xiang*.

All of the languages are tonal—that is the meaning of many individual words is based on the tone used in pronouncing them. Furthermore, the languages and many of the dialects are different enough that they are mutually unintelligible.

Despite the fact that the vocabulary and pronunciation of these languages and "dialects" differ fundamentally, they are all written with exactly the same ideographic characters. The characters are simply pronounced differently in the case of each language and dialect.

While the Chinese who are not multilingual cannot understand the other dialects when they are spoken, they can read and understand them when they are written. In other words, the Chinese can read all of the major languages of the country fluently without being able to speak them in the local language or dialect.

Over the ages, this remarkable development was the primary factor that made it possible for the Han culture to spread throughout the eastern and central regions of China, and still today is one of the main elements that ties the Chinese people together.

Shortly after the revolutionary communist leader Mao Zedong and his party took over China in the fall of 1949 he decreed that Mandarin, the language of the Beijing area, should become the national language of the whole country and mandated that it be taught in all schools. (The effort to make Mandarin the official language of China first began in 1913 but was unsuccessful because of political and social disruptions.)

This farsighted policy has resulted in most Chinese in the provinces and regions outside of Beijing speaking some, if not fluent, Mandarin.

Mandarin Chinese has only four tones (the others have up to eight tones) and is therefore the easiest of the "dialects" for foreigners to master.

Writing Chinese in Roman Letters

The official Chinese system of writing the national language in Roman letters, *pinyin* (peen-een), or "Roman transcription," was made the law of the land on February 11, 1958 by the communist government. It is said that over one billion Chinese now know how to write and read Romanized versions of the national language—a remarkable phenomenon that has been extraordinarily beneficial to the internationalization of both the Chinese economy and the culture.

This phenomenon has been even more beneficial to foreign residents and visitors to China who cannot read the traditional ideograms used to write the language—especially its use for public signs.

Unfortunately for English speakers and most other Westerners, the official system for writing Chinese words in Roman letters is not based on Roman or English phonetics. It is based on Mandarin phonetics, some of which differ significantly from English sounds. Thus the term for China, Zhongguo, is pronounced Johhng-gwah.

The word for Mandarin, Putonghua, is pronounced Poo-tuung-hwah, which means "Common Language." The word for toilet, cesuo, is pronounced t'sue-soh. The word for please, qing, is pronounced cheeng, and so on.

Pronunciation Guide

(Here is the official phonetic alphabet for Mandarin)

Pinyin	As in:	Pinyin	As in:
a	far	p	par
b	be	q	cheek
c	as the ts in its	r	rzh
ch	church	s	so
d	do	sh	shore
e	her	t	top
ei	way	u	too
f	foot	v	used only in foreign words and some dialects
g	go	w	want
h	her	x	she
i	eat	y	yet
j	jeep	z	zoo (zu)
k	kind	zh	Cj (as in jump)
l	land		
m	me		
n	no		
o	law		

Here are some useful words and phrases in Romanized Mandarin with their phonetic equivalents as an example of how Chinese is pronounced:

Ni hao (nee how) = which may be used for all of the following: hello, good morning, good afternoon, and good evening

Ni hao ma? (nee how mah?) = How are you?

Xie xie (shay shay) = Thank you

Gui xing? (ghway sheeng?) = What is your name?

Wo jiao .... (wah jee-ow ....) = My name is ....

PREFACE

The Origin of Cultures

Cultures have, of course, evolved over time through a synthesizing process of geography, climate, survival methods, primitive spiritual beliefs, social choices and finally sophisticated philosophical beliefs.

In more modern times science and technology have become major contributors to cultures, making them far more dynamic and transforming them in ways that could not have been imagined in earlier times.

Science and technology are also homogenizing the world's leading cultures in ways and at speeds that are more like science fiction than traditional reality.

The end results of all these factors are the unique cultures that exist today—all of which, despite fundamental ongoing changes, especially in modern times, still retain much of their traditional power.

Traditional ways of thinking and doing things are, of course, the most prevalent in Western societies that for millennia have been under the influence of powerful god-based religions—Judaism, Christianity and Islam...and in Eastern countries that have been under the influence of Buddhism, Confucianism, and Taoism.

The power of traditional cultures today is based on whether or not the people are spiritually and politically free to think and behave as individuals.

Societies that have traditionally had—and still have—powerful authoritarian governments and religions, with little or no personal choice in the beliefs and behavior of the people, continue to be the most traditional in their thinking and acting.

The imposition of a communist style government on China in 1949, the so-called Cultural Revolution that occurred between 1966 and 1976, and the gradual adoption of a capitalistic market economy following the destructive debacle of the cultural revolution led to fundamental changes in the culture of China, and it is still a work in progress—part traditional Chinese, part modern Chinese, and part Western.

Boyé Lafayette De Mente

INTRODUCTION

The Foundation of Chinese Culture

Many people today still mistakenly regard the arts and crafts of individual societies as their "culture." Arts and crafts *reflect* culture but they do not create it and they do not transmit it. You can view, collect, and study Chinese, Japanese or Inuit artifacts all your life and you will not become fully conversant with the cultures that created them.

The Yin-Yang Principle in Chinese Culture

The Chinese terms yin and yang are generally known as relating to such opposites as hot-cold, sweet-sour, male-female, and positive-negative. But this view is incomplete. The yin-yang concept is, in fact, the foundation of all cultures—a concept that to my knowledge has never before been associated with cultures within or outside of the Chinese sphere of influence.

The principle of yin and yang is, in fact, an explanation of the behavior of all organic and inorganic things in the universe, as well as the invisible energy that infuses the cosmos down to the level of quantum physics. The concept incorporates the creation, interaction, and extinction of all things in an unending cycle.

Several of the most basic elements of the culture of China (as well as the cultures of Japanese and Korean)—including all personal and business relationships—are precise manifestations of the yin-yang principle.

Looking just below the surface of Chinese, Japanese, and Korean behavior reveals that the yin-yang principle applies to all relationships between males and females, between seniors and juniors, between the government and the private sector—in fact, to all relationships and all activities, including the food the Chinese eat and the order in which the individual dishes are consumed.

Chinese scholars and philosophers have been writing about the yin-yang principle since around 1,400 B.C. But long before that they had become acutely aware that the yin-yang relationships between things and people are not fixed, that they are in a constant state of flux and that they wax and wane in inverse proportions.

And the point is that not only the cultures of Asians but all other cultures are based on trying to keep all yin-yang relationships in harmony.

But cultural harmony does not mean or infer equality in relationships. It means only that the relationships are on a level that is acceptable or bearable to the parties concerned—whether or not they like them, or how disadvantageous they might be.

Incredibly, businesspeople and world leaders alike have only recently become painfully aware that ignoring the cultures of others is unwise and dangerous. Now—finally—the importance of understanding cultures is a new mantra for business leaders as well as diplomats and some politicians.

For most people becoming familiar with the cultures of others has been and still is a process that requires long periods of living in and personally experiencing the cultures.

However, as noted above, there is an easier and faster way of coming to fully understand and appreciate other cultures, and that is through my "cultural code word" approach, which makes it possible for you to get into and understand the mindset of other people more easily and quickly.

China's famous yin and yang "code words" provide an extraordinary example of the advantage of using culturally pregnant terms and phrases as doorways to the culture of the country.

In a very fundamental sense the yin-yang principle of China incorporates the essence and the heart Chinese culture—socially, economically, and politically—and I believe it is impossible to fully understand the culture without a comprehensive knowledge of this ancient concept.

The Chinese yin-yang view of human relations as situational is not always fair in the Western sense but it is realistic in that in nature *absolute* equality exists only in relative terms and only for very short periods of time.

Chinese culture is now evolving in the direction of Western cultures—especially popular American culture. More and more Chinese are giving preference to personal, people-oriented standards that are making their society less formalistic, less ritualistic, and less homogenous. But it is still Chinese!

In this book I have attempted to pinpoint areas of China's traditional values and behavior that continue to play a significant role in the business and social relationships of the Chinese, as well as to identify key areas of Chinese culture that have changed as a result of the adoption of a market-based economy and other elements of American and other Western cultures.

I have also included an extensive selection of Chinese "code words" that explain the essence and role of key elements of the traditional culture that have survived into modern times and continue to define the national character of the Chinese.

In the 13th century China was known as one of the world's best travel destinations not only because of its unique culture but also because of the Chinese custom of extending extraordinary hospitality to foreign visitors; the tolerance with which the Chinese accepted and treated foreign visitors who were not conversant with their culture, and the extraordinary friendliness of the people—especially the young.

That China is back—with many improvements in the physical amenities that are now available to visitors and businesspeople, from hotels and restaurants to high-speed trains.

DISCUSSION TOPICS & QUESTIONS

The Yin and Yang of Life

1. The old saying that the only things in life that are inevitable are taxes and death has a grain of truth, but it does not provide sufficient framework for fully understanding the nature of life, or for all of the options that people have for making their lives the best that they can be. Understanding the yin-yang principle provides much of this framework.

2. Assuming this premise, would you suggest that the principle of yin-yang be clearly taught in schools around the world?

3. Why have the Chinese not been able to take full advantage of their knowledge of the yin-yang principle—historically as well as today?

4. What are the political ramifications of people being able to make the choices inherent in the yin-yang principle?

PART I

The Role of Language in Preserving & Transmitting Chinese Culture

What most of mankind has missed over the millennia has been the relationship between language and culture. Languages are, in fact, the repository as well as the transmitter of cultures. Languages contain the essence, the tone, the flavor, and the spirit of cultures, and serve as doorways to understanding them.

The influence that languages have on the values, attitudes, and behavior of people is fundamental, and is one of the primary reasons why the present-day world is in a constant state of turmoil. We cannot communicate fully and effectively across the cultural barriers inherent in languages and the mindsets they create and sustain.

It is, of course, fairly simple to interpret or translate technical subjects from one language into another, but translating cultural attitudes and values into another language ranges from difficult to impossible. The translations may be perfectly correct as far as the words are concerned, but they seldom if ever include all of the cultural nuances that are bound up in the words and are the essence of the original language.

Not being relatively fluent in the native language of a people means that you are barred from entering their cultural circle—from understanding and expressing thoughts with the same essence, the same tone and the same flavor that is inherent in their language. I have said this is like taking a shower while wearing a waterproof suit.

And it goes without saying that the spirit of a people is also bound up in their language—in key words that are pregnant with cultural content.

Any attempt to truly understand the character and personality of Chinese, Germans, Japanese, Koreans, Mexicans, or any other group of people—to put yourself in their shoes, as the saying goes—must include a deep knowledge of the cultural essences of their languages, and this is a challenge facing mankind that cannot be easily or quickly resolved.

During my early years as a trade journalist in Asia the deeper I got into the Japanese, Korean, and Chinese way of thinking and doing things the more obvious it became that they were culturally programmed and controlled by key words in their languages, and that these words provided a short-cut to understanding them.

Because the values and behavior of people in all societies, especially older societies, are fundamentally controlled by their languages, learning the meaning and everyday use of key words in their languages is faster and often far more effective in understanding their culture than reading treatises by anthropologists and sociologists.

DISCUSSION TOPICS & QUESTIONS

The Ignorance Factor in Human Affairs
1. Throughout history, and to a great extent still today, humanity in general has either been ignorant of—or has chosen to ignore—the relationship between languages and cultures, a factor that has contributed enormously to the conflicts that have plagued mankind from day one.

2. How did China, with its diverse collection of languages and dialects, overcome many of the cultural, political, and social prob-

lems associated with multiple indigenous languages? Do you favor multiple languages in your own country? Why?

3. Do you believe that the early Chinese solution to this problem remains a serious detriment to the ability of the central government to carry out its policies? Explain.

The Role of *Hanzi* (Hahn-jee) in Chinese Culture

It was not just Confucianism, Daoism, other philosophies and the political power of China's kings and emperors that helped meld the diverse Chinese groups into a single nation. It was also the power of language—especially the Chinese system of writing with ideographs, called *Han zi* (Hahn jee), or "Chinese characters." (By official choice this is usually written in Roman letters as a single word: *Hanzi*.)

Hanzi "characters" originated as pictorial drawings that were already in use in China over 3,000 years ago, first being used on animal bones, tortoise shells, and earthenware. Archeologists have discovered such ancient objects bearing more than 4,600 individual characters. Over time, these drawings became more and more stylized, and by 1000 B.C. had evolved into the ideograms that are known today.

During this evolution the number of ideographs grew to some 60,000, most of which can still be seen in ancient books and on a variety of artifacts. The famous *Kwangxi* dictionary lists 47,031 characters.

But only 3,500 to 4,000 of the characters are necessary for complete literacy in present-day China. Each of the characters represents a syllable or word, and words consist of one, two, three, or more characters.

Unlike the Roman letters used to represent the English language, which have no meaning by themselves, China's now uniformly stylized ideograms represent an actual pictorial image of things, concepts, and even sounds, and are therefore "alive" with meanings that go back to the dawn of Chinese civilization.

Because the meanings of the pictographs were universal they were absorbed into the cultures of all of China's ethnic groups no matter what dialect or language they spoke. As a result of this, all of the diverse ethnic groups of China had a common means of communicating.

This meant that all educated Chinese throughout the immense country could read whatever was written in the characters, an extraordinary phenomenon that went far beyond the use and influence of Latin in the Western world.

Because the characters literally represented the objects and concepts that made up the Chinese concept of the cosmos, the people and the social, political, and spiritual environment in which they lived, the *Hanzi* became the repository of the culture of mainstream China and the primary vehicle by which the culture was transmitted from one educated generation to the next.

Until the advent of modern times, large numbers of China's upper classes spent years memorizing the readings of several thousand *Hanzi* and learning how to write them with considerable skill. Being able to draw the *Hanzi* with professional skill became a hallmark of the cultural standing of an individual, and was often a requirement for success in a number of fields.

Learning to read and draw even 3,000 characters has a profound influence on the character of the Chinese. It addition to gaining considerable physical dexterity with their hands, they are also conditioned to recognize forms and relationships and to think about things and do things in a precise, methodical manner.

One has only to contrast learning how to read and write the 26 letters of the Roman alphabet with learning how to read and draw 3,000 Chinese ideograms, some of which have over 20 strokes that must be done in the right way and in the right order, to begin to appreciate the impact such physical and mental conditioning has on the character and personality of the Chinese.

In fact, many of the more admirable skills and traits the Chinese have as artists and workers in various fields are due in part, if not wholly, to their *Hanzi* training.

Still today the *Hanzi* are the tie that binds China's ethnic and linguistic groups together, especially in a cultural sense. And now that literacy in China is well above the norm for most countries the power of the characters is more widespread and more influential than ever before. But despite this, there is a bad as well as a good side to the language and *Hanzi*.

On the good side *Hanzi* gave the Chinese a cultural mutuality and coherence that historically was one of their strongest points. But when they began to encounter Westerners with their diverse cultures the very things that had made their language and writing system such an asset suddenly became a major obstacle.

Both the spoken form and the written form of the language held the people of China and their culture firmly in their grip until near the end of the 20th century—binding them to beliefs and behavior that were totally incompatible with a capitalistic, consumer oriented, democratic society.

The imperatives of thinking and acting differently to cope with the demands of capitalism and consumerism were, in fact, one of the primary reasons why the culture of younger generations of Chinese changed so rapidly, including creating their own slang and way of using the language.

DISCUSSION TOPICS & QUESTIONS

Hanzi vs. the Roman Alphabet

1. Given the fact that that there is a negative side to learning and using *Hanzi* would you advocate that the Chinese people give up using the characters to write their language and adopt the culturally neutral Roman letter system?

2. Since each Chinese character has an inherent meaning of its own, while the words formed by letters of the Roman alphabet are meaningless until they are given an arbitrary meaning, would you agree that the ideograms are an inherently superior method of communicating in writing and that the Chinese should continue using the *Hanzi* system? Explain your position.

3. Do you foresee the possibility that the people of China will gradually switch from writing their language with the ideogram characters to using Roman letters?

4. What could the ramifications be of such a dramatic change in the acculturation of the Chinese and in their relations with the rest of the world?

5. Would you recommend that the Chinese government prohibit the formal and/or official use of Roman letters when writing their language? Explain your rationale.

The Chinese Language under Assault

A major part of the influence that a country has beyond its borders is seen in its language—to what degree it is studied and used by other people, and in particular to how much of its underlying philosophy becomes assimilated into other cultures.

Now that China has joined the world community as an economic and political superpower the role and importance of the Chinese language is following the same historical path. Millions of people around the world are now studying the Chinese language and a number of key Chinese words have already became a part of the world language—a number that will continue to grow for the foreseeable future.

Chinese terms that have also been a part of the world culture for several generations include yin-yang, feng shui, kung fu and mahjong. News media around the world now routinely use a number of key business-related Chinese words that has added them to the world language.

At present, one of the best known and most used of these terms is *guanxi* (gwahn-she), which refers to the network of personal connections that are an essential part of all business and personal relationships in China. This book identifies and defines several dozen other key Chinese "code words" that are culturally revealing and will no doubt become a part of the world language in the future.

As said, however, the fundamental relationship between language and the character and spirit of a people has not yet been fully recognized or appreciated by most people. This ignorance of the role of language in the character, spirit, and culture of a people has resulted in both the languages and cultures of more advanced nations, particularly the United States and Japan, being debased to the point that there is a serious cultural and linguistic gap between the generations.

Elements of China's traditional mainstream culture are, in fact, also being eroded daily—a phenomenon that is demonstrated and promoted by the abuse and misuse of the Chinese language among the younger generations, and the news and entertainment media that caters to them.

This linguistic and cultural gap is becoming increasingly obvious in China. The use of virtually all dialects and languages in China, particularly Mandarin, the primary language, is changing—and these changes are reflected in the mainstream as well as the regional and ethnic cultures.

The United States is a glaring example of the erosion of its language and culture, and may provide a stark example to the Chinese. Mainstream Americans in particular have traditionally been insensitive to the languages and cultures of others and seem oblivious to what is happening to their own.

This same malady could also envelop China as its economic and political power increases, but there is hope that the Chinese will be able to avoid this cultural myopia because of the knowledge they have accumulated over their 5,000-year history.

In the long run, the Chinese understanding of human nature and the cultural devices they have created to deal effectively with this nature may give them an advantage over societies with religious-based cultures that are often incompatible with human needs and aspirations.

Chinese culture is not the most traditional or the most hidebound of the world's cultures, and like all cultures it is susceptible to incredible changes in a very short period of time—changes that were unthinkable until the weakening of both Confucianism and Communism.

Given the economic and political roles that China is now play-ing in world affairs—and the fact that the importance of this role is increasing daily—understanding and learning how to interface with China economically, politically, *and* socially—even without knowledge of the language—is of vital importance for the world at large.

DISCUSSION TOPICS & QUESTIONS

The Influence of English on Chinese Culture

1. The cultural content of the English language is profoundly dif-ferent from the cultural content of the Chinese language, and it is having a significant influence on the attitudes and behavior of people who study it.

2. Much of the cultural content of English is destructive to the traditional Chinese way of thinking and expressing themselves because it is based on different values and different ways of thinking.

3. In earlier times the Chinese government did not approve of its people learning foreign languages because they did not want their culture "polluted" by foreign beliefs and concepts. Now, millions of Chinese are studying English. What does this tell you about the Chinese mindset and the policies of China's leaders?

4. The study of English is one of the primary elements in bring-ing about the dramatic changes one sees in the way the Chi-nese think and behave.

5. The Chinese government attempts to block the negative influence that the English language brings with it, but without success.

6. Do you believe that English should become the second language of China? Why? What benefits would this bring to China? What would the negative impact be?

7. If you spoke Chinese fluently and were interacting with a Chinese who could speak and understand English fairly well, which language would you choose to use? Why?

8. Do you believe one can truly understand the Chinese mindset without being fluent in the Chinese language? Explain your view.

9. Do you believe it would be a good idea for English-speaking countries to be more direct and more forceful in spreading the use of English around the world? Explain your reasoning.

PART II

The Essence of China's Traditional Culture

China's rapid rise to economic and political super-powerdom following the death of Mao Zedong in 1976 was a seminal event in the lives of the Chinese. For the first time in the history of the country ordinary people were freed from most of the cultural and political shackles that had prevented them from using their abilities to help themselves.

During the Mao regime (1949-1976) the independent and entrepreneurial efforts of the Chinese were generally limited to small-scale activities, many of them underground, because the government attempted to control every aspect and element of the economy. With the death of Mao and a significant switch to a market economy all of the long-repressed talents and ambitions of vast numbers of Chinese were quickly channeled into entrepreneurial enterprises. Hundreds of thousands of businesses sprang up virtually overnight.

The economic success of China following the fall of the barriers against private enterprise became a stake in the heart of the communist ideology, and speaks for itself. But despite the American and Western façade that now blankets much of China many of the elements that made up the traditional character of the people continue to exist and to thrive.

There were, of course, several fundamental and well-known sources that contributed to the traditional mindset of the Chinese—beginning with primitive folk beliefs that were eventually

followed by the sophisticated philosophies of Buddhism, Confucianism, Taoism, and Zen.

These sources impregnated the Chinese mind with the values,
ethics, and etiquette that became the foundation of their national
character, which more than three thousand years ago contributed
to their creation of a civilization that in many ways was the most
advanced in the world.

However, in the early years of the 15th century some of these
same influences resulted in the imperial Chinese government halt-
ing its encouragement of innovation and progress—a move that
was to have disastrous results for China for the next 500 years.

Blinded by the past achievements of their ancestors and cap-
tivated by their insular outlook toward the rest of the world, the
Imperial Court in the 15th century announced that there was
nothing in the rest of the world that China needed or wanted, and
that nothing need be changed. Emphasizing the past and maintaining the status quo became the official policy. Change became
virtually taboo.

While the Industrial Revolution in Europe changed the outside
world and turned several European countries into empire build-
ers at the expense of the Americas and most of Asia, China stag-
nated and was eventually roiled by foreign invasions and revolutions that did not end until 1949 when the Communist Party
under Chairman Mao Zedong took over the country.

DISCUSSION TOPICS & QUESTIONS

Destroying Old China to Save It

1. The powerful hold of China's traditional culture prevented
   the country from joining in the Industrial Revolution when it
   began in England in the mid-1700s.

2. Among other forces that conspired against China to prevent
   the country from industrializing until the 20th century were
   the colonial ideologies that developed in European countries

following the discovery of the North and South American continents at the end of the 15th century.

3. China itself came very close to being completely colonized by European powers in the 19th century. When it resisted these moves the U.S. and European powers invaded the country under a variety of pretexts. In the late 1800s Japan followed the example of the Western powers by invading Korea and Manchuria and soon thereafter annexing both of them. This was a prelude to Japan's invasion of China in the 1930s and the Japanese attack on Hawaii in 1941.

4. These events led to the United States allying with Chinese Nationalists in an attempt to defeat the Japanese and drive them out of China...which in turn led to a revolutionary war between the Nationalists and the new Communist Party under Mao Zedong before World War II ended in 1945—a war that the Nationalists and their American ally lost in 1949.

5. As we have seen, after Mao took control of China he attempted to destroy its traditional culture in order to transform it into an economic and military bastion that could protect itself from the colonial powers. Does this fact change your view of him?

China's Vertical Society

The hierarchical social and political arrangement of people is as old as the human race, and nowhere was this power-based custom more assiduously practiced than in Confucian-oriented China.

Confucius advocated precisely arranged divisions of society as a means of achieving and maintaining social and political harmony, and his teachings were to prevail in China until the mid-1900s.

Mao Zedong, whose communist creed was ostensibly based on social and economic equality, attempted to eliminate this ancient Confucian philosophy from Chinese society during his 28-year reign but he was only partially successful.

The political, social, and economic reforms that followed Mao's death were more successful than Mao in reducing the role of hierarchy in Chinese life, but it still exists and is of vital importance.

While economic power and wealth are now virtually guaranteed to vault previously low or middle-class Chinese into the ranks of the social elite, the vast majority of Chinese still exist in a society characterized by class and rank.

All Chinese and foreigners alike must take into account the role and importance of social classes and hierarchical rank in business as well as in government in present-day China. Not surprisingly, rank is more important to government officials than it is to businesspeople.

DISCUSSION TOPICS & QUESTIONS

The Role of Communism in the Remaking China

1. Mao Zedong became a communist because he realized that to change the traditional mindset and behavior of the Chinese quickly would require the absolute power that is part of the communist ideology.

2. Mao was determined to remake China in the communist image because he believed that was the only way to prevent the country from being colonized by foreign powers.

3. Many of the changes mandated by Mao, such as giving women the right to vote, were, in fact, reforms that have not yet been achieved in many other countries. Do you believe this mitigates the harsh measures he used in his attempts to change the thinking and behavior of the people?

4. Mao also believed that it was necessary to completely break the hold that Confucianism had on the people of China before the country could be modernized.

5. Because of frustration with the slow progress being made in his efforts to modernize China Mao unleashed his "Red Guards" (millions of high school and university students), with orders to destroy the Confucian order of China and "re-educate" the educated and the urban middle class by trial and by exiling them to the countryside where they had to survive on their own. This so-called "Cultural Revolution" began in 1966 and lasted until 1976 when Mao died. Altogether it caused the death of some 20 million people. Do you believe the growing prosperity and personal freedom that the Chinese are now experiencing justifies this tragic episode in the history of the country?

6. The Communist Party of China, particularly through its military forces, owns and controls a significant percentage of all the larger companies in the country. Should this prevent foreign companies from doing business in China?

7. Should foreign companies relax their ethical standards in order to do business with Chinese companies—something many of them have been accused of doing?

8. One of the ploys that the Chinese government and Chinese companies continue to use to get special advantages in dealing with foreign governments and foreign companies is to insist that the foreign entities "owe China" because of historical factors. Do you believe it is ethical for the foreign side to give in to this kind of pressure?

9. One of the main reasons why China's leaders were able to transform the country into an economic powerhouse in such a short period of time was that they did not allow religious beliefs to interfere with their policies. On the other hand, the cultural, economic, and social progress of many Western and Near East countries is impeded by the influence of religions. Do you believe that these countries would be better off if this religious influence was eliminated?

The Role of Situational Ethics

There are, in fact, three categories of ethics in China: traditional Chinese ethics, Western ethics, and Communist ethics. Which one is engaged at a particularly time depends upon the circumstances and the people involved.

Communist ethics often—but certainly not always—prevail on high government levels. The further one gets away from the central government, and the lower the ranking, the less likely the ethical guidelines will be communist.

In the business world in particular as well as increasingly on lower and mid levels of government, Western ethics are the standards by which a growing number of people conduct their relationships.

But all things considered, traditional Chinese ethics—which are situational in nature—continue to play a leading role in most of the affairs and policies of individual Chinese as well as government officials on all levels.

By traditional/situational ethics, I mean a flexible standard of thought and behavior that is based on the circumstances at hand, real or imagined, instead of universal principles.

This gives the Chinese a tremendous amount of leeway in what they regard as right or wrong, acceptable or unacceptable—a position or stand that can drive logic-and-ethic driven Westerners up the proverbial wall.

The Chinese preference and use of situational ethics is a product of their past, when individuals did not have absolute rights that were protected either by law or by custom and were subject to the arbitrary rule of their superiors, including family members and government officials on all levels.

In such authoritarian societies right is what those in power say it is, and is something that they can change any time they want to. This results in people giving whatever answer they believe is right for the circumstance at hand—that will be the least likely to get them into trouble or simply inconvenience them in some way.

Foreign businesspeople and diplomats dealing with China should keep the role of situational ethics in mind in all of their relationships because things are often not what they are said to be, or seem to be.

DISCUSSION TOPICS & QUESTIONS

The Advantages of Situational Ethics

1. When Westerners first encountered the Chinese and began initiating trade and diplomatic relations with them they often complained that the Chinese had no ethics, no morality—that they assumed whatever stance that was the most advantageous to them. Situational ethics had, in fact, become the standard in ancient China because there was no body of laws to protect the people in their dealings with the government and with each other. Do you see this mindset and behavior, today, in the U.S. and other countries of the world?

2. By basing their behavior on the situation at hand the Chinese and other Asians often have a significant advantage over Westerners who attempt to follow principles of fairness and equitability in their relationships. Do you believe that Western companies and countries should relax their standards in order to deal with the Chinese on an even footing?

3. Chinese businesspeople and government officials can be ruthless in their efforts to benefit themselves and the country. Generally speaking, Westerners equate such ruthlessness with unethical and immoral behavior. How would you suggest that this philosophical difference be handled by Westerners?

4. What guidelines would you suggest that Western businesspeople and diplomats use when their Chinese counterparts demand access to proprietary information and technology?

5. Establishing personal relationships with individual Chinese is often the only way that Westerners can surmount cultural differences and succeed in dealing fairly and effectively with each other. And yet, Americans in particular want and attempt to cut deals in a matter of hours or days after the first meeting. What does this say about Americans and American culture as opposed to the Chinese and their culture?

6. Situational ethics are, in fact, becoming more and more common in the West. Do you think this is a good trend? If not, how would you go about stopping the trend altogether—or at least slowing it down?

The Preference for "Soft No's"

Just plain "yes" and "no" are seldom used by Chinese and other Asians, and this can cause serious problems for Westerners. There are, of course, fundamental cultural reasons for this behavior.

Traditionally such blunt responses as yes and no were considered impolite. But even more important was that fact that speaking in clear, precise terms could be dangerous. Speaking in vague terms was a way of surviving.

In ordinary conversation Chinese (as well as Japanese and Koreans) customarily express the concept of yes and no by using the positives and negatives of verbs, often in vague ways if the situation is sensitive.

It has been said by both Chinese and foreigners who have had long experience in China that there are no words for "yes" and "no" in Chinese. There are, but they are seldom used.

Throughout Chinese history giving unequivocal answers or responses to people, especially direct superiors and others in positions of power, could have grave results if anything went wrong. The possibility of things going wrong eventually led the people to simply avoid all direct yes and no responses, to the point that such behavior became ingrained in both Chinese ethics and etiquette.

This led to the development of what has been described as "soft no's"—meaning no in a roundabout and often obtuse way that was unlikely to give offense or disappoint. Often times these no's are so obtuse that foreigners do not recognize them.

Soft no's are still especially common in business and political relationships in China, so it is important for foreigners to have their antenna up and finely tuned in their dealings with Chinese—keeping in mind that such responses are not necessarily meant to be misleading or malicious, but they can be both when unscrupulous people are involved.

There are numerous occasions, however, when it is vital to get a clear yes or no. On these occasions it is often necessary to be creative in framing and posing questions until the real answer becomes clear.

DISCUSSION TOPICS & QUESTIONS

The Chinese Way of Communicating

1. Historically in China there was no such thing as a Bill of Rights for people. Without either customs or laws to protect them, and being subject to arbitrary punishment by seniors and officials, the only way they could partially protect themselves was to scrupulously avoid being honest and candid in their speech.

   Over the generations this situation had a profound influence on Chinese culture, particularly in the etiquette controlling their behavior in all of their relationships, both public and private.

2. The traditionally extreme sensitivity of the Chinese to speech, not only in the manner of speaking but in the vocabulary as well, has diminished significantly in today's China, particularly among the younger generations in personal and private relationships, but it is still an important factor in most public affairs of whatever kind. Would you advocate that Westerners, again Americans in particular, be especially circumspect in their interactions with Chinese?

3. In business and diplomatic negotiations in China how would you go about making your points clearly, completely, and quickly without upsetting your Chinese counterparts?

4. Under what circumstances do you think it would be advisable, and acceptable, for foreigners to adopt the Chinese way when interacting with them?

The Chinese Way of Viewing & Using Laws

This is another aspect of Chinese culture that can be confusing to foreigners. Until modern times China did not have a detailed body of laws or regulations that prescribed expected or accepted behavior and provided for sanctions to be applied when these laws were broken.

There were a variety of imperial expectations, positions, and edicts that had developed and become institutionalized over the centuries, but not a body of laws or a justice system similar to what exists in most Western countries today.

Instead of the Western type of system Chinese officials on all levels were empowered by custom and by imperial mandates to serve as judge and jury in all actions and disputes. That is, officials decided what was right and what was wrong, and decided on any punishment to be meted out.

People knew from long experience what was and was not acceptable and because punishments for even minor offenses could be fatal they tended to be exceptionally well-behaved.

This approach, which was advocated by the great sage Confucius and other early Chinese philosophers, was based on the presumption that if there are no precise, public laws, and if punishments for misbehaving are swift and severe, people will be even more circumspect in their behavior than otherwise.

China now has a fairly large body of detailed laws that apply nationally, regionally, and locally, but not nearly as many or as detailed as is the case in the U.S. and elsewhere.

Furthermore, the ancient concept of limiting laws and keeping some of them secret is still practiced on all levels of government. In addition to not making all of the laws and regulations public, officials on all levels still have or assume the power to make or ignore regulations, and to interpret existing laws as they see fit.

Governments on all levels also issue edicts that most people ignore because they disagree with them, in which case the government agency or ministry concerned will often back off, explaining that the new laws were just a test.

National, provincial, and city governments are gradually increasing the number of laws they have to contend with modern circumstances, but generally speaking these laws do not always compare or equate with Western laws pertaining to the same situations.

This often puts foreign businesses and other foreign interests in an awkward position because there are many occasions when they cannot anticipate when or how the laws are going to be enforced.

In other words, laws in China often have a personal element in what they cover and how they are interpreted and used. This means that foreigners engaging in business or diplomatic affairs in China must take into account the personal nature of the laws and their enforcement.

Knowing how to live with and work within the various legal frameworks that exist in China requires a great deal of cultural knowledge and experience.

People who do not have this knowledge and experience are strongly advised to engage the help of local consultants in addition to making a special point of developing and keeping close relationships with all of the government officials who have any jurisdiction over their areas of interest.

And there are specific protocols for developing and keeping such relationships. (See the key word concepts in Part III.)

DISCUSSION TOPICS & QUESTIONS

Customs vs. Laws

1. Until recent times, Chinese behavior was mostly controlled by customs and philosophical beliefs rather than laws. Contrast this system with the rule of law that gradually developed in the West.

2. Generally speaking, today's Chinese are still not comfortable with abiding by laws designed to control both their private and public behavior. They still tend to consider laws an infringement on their rights. List areas and ways this attitude could impact on the conduct of business and politics, and suggest

constructive ways that Westerners might respond to make the best of the situation.

3. How would you go about convincing a potential Chinese partner to abide by the laws of *your* country—laws that determine what you can and cannot do?

4. How would you avoid getting caught up in illegal activities by a Chinese partner?

The Chinese Concept of Time

Another cultural factor that foreigners dealing with China should be aware of—and know how to use—is the traditional Chinese concept of time. In simple terms, Westerners are programmed to think of time as passing in a straight line into the future, and looking upon the past as gone forever. The Chinese have traditionally been conditioned to think of time as moving in a circle, with the present always connected to the past, making the past therefore something that cannot be ignored.

This difference often has a profound impact on formal Chinese and Western relationships, and can be the source of misunderstanding and conflict. Differences between the way the Chinese and Westerners react to this cultural dichotomy can range from very conspicuous and very loud to very subtle—in which case they may not become apparent for some time.

This is another situation where knowledge of Chinese culture and experience in working within it effectively are very important to both businesspeople and foreign diplomats dealing with China.

There are numerous elements to this time factor—elements that range from the age of the individuals involved, whether or not the Chinese side speaks English and/or has had experience dealing with Westerners in or outside of China, to the gender of the individuals.

I discuss many of these elements in the "cultural code words" in Part III of this book.

DISCUSSION TOPICS & QUESTIONS

Time Moves in a Circle

1. Prior to the development of capitalistic and consumer oriented systems the Chinese viewed time as moving in a circular fashion rather than passing in a straight line, as is the view of the Western world. Government officials and bureaucrats in particular also tended to move slowly and to think in terms of decades—not months or even years.

2. A great many Chinese in private industry now work at breakneck speed and seem incapable of slowing down, and even bureaucrats move faster than they did in the past. However, the traditional concept of time as moving in a circle is still discernible in much of the behavior of the Chinese and must be taken into consideration.

3. Do you perceive the traditional Chinese version of time as having merit—as often being more realistic than the Western view?

4. What are some of the most obvious advantages in having a long-range circular view rather than a short-range view that is often not planned well and does not allow for changes that cannot be foreseen?

Emotional Intelligence vs. Rational Intelligence

Another cultural difference between the East and West that plays a vital role in relationships between individuals and between companies as well as in world affairs across the board can be summed up in the concepts of "emotional intelligence" and "rational intelligence."

In broad terms, Western thinking and behaving is based on rational intelligence—that is on facts and objective logical thinking, whereas traditional Chinese thinking and behaving was/is based on emotional factors first and rational factors later—if ever.

Apparently it was not until around the end of the 20th century that someone in the West came up with the specific terms "emotional intelligence" and "rational intelligence".

In short, the Chinese were conditioned for millennia to think and behave on the basis of personal and emotional considerations—not hard impersonal and unemotional factors. In that culture, emotional intelligence took precedence over rational intelligence.

To Westerners the thought of applying emotional intelligence to their personal relationships with their spouses, children, or friends, etc., makes pretty good sense up to a point. But the thought of taking an emotional approach to business and political affairs is enough to induce a state of shock in most of them.

Despite the millennia of conditioning in giving emotional and personal considerations precedence in their daily affairs— by imperial law and by custom—the Chinese retained the ability to think in rational, logical, and pragmatic terms because these characteristics were absolutely essential to their survival.

The role of emotional intelligence in China did not begin to change dramatically until after the death of Mao Zedong in 1976 and his replacement by the pragmatic Deng Xiaoping, who shortly thereafter visited the city of Shenzhen near Hong Kong and was astounded to see that it had become a prosperous and thriving example of capitalism and entrepreneurship unlike anything else in the country. Not long afterward, Deng began touting his "to get rich is glorious" slogan and set China on the course that would change it—and the world!

This phenomenon resulted in a great clash with the traditional role of emotional intelligence in China because it was fundamentally incompatible with many of the Western business concepts that prevailed at that time. The more Westernized business management in China became the smaller the role of emotional intelligence.

Rational intelligence has continued to gain ground in China, in both business and government, but it has not displaced emotional intelligence as an integral part of Chinese culture. The vast majority of ordinary Chinese still react emotionally first, and then, when necessary, engage the rational side of their brains.

Westerners engaging with the Chinese, especially in business and diplomacy, should be aware of the traditional and present-day role of emotional intelligence in China because it continues to have an impact on their thinking and behavior.

While the importance of rational intelligence in China continues to grow there is virtually no possibility that it will totally replace emotional intelligence.

In fact, in the last decades of the 20th century Western business leaders themselves began to pick up on the importance of emotional intelligence in management and to change their personnel management policies accordingly—primarily because of serious competition from Japan that resulted in them studying and adopting some of the emotional intelligence elements from Japanese culture.

American and European corporations that changed the culture of their management because of competition from Japan won't know what real competition is until China reaches even half of its potential.

DISCUSSION TOPICS & QUESTIONS

The Importance of Emotional Intelligence

1. The Chinese, Japanese, and other Asians have long given emotional intelligence precedence over hard facts and fact-based thinking and behavior, which have long been the bedrock of the cultures of English speaking countries in particular. Contrast these two cultural mindsets.

2. The experience and expertise of Chinese and other Asians in using emotional intelligence often gives them a decided advantage in dealing with Westerners. Why is this so, how do you think it manifests itself, and how would you counter it?

3. By combining the elements of Confucianism with both emotional and factual intelligence, the Chinese created one of the world's most powerful and enduring cultures.

4. Why has both factual and emotional intelligence been ignored for so long in Christian and Islamic societies as opposed to life in China?

The Chinese "What" vs. the Western "Why/Because"

Another dichotomy in Chinese and Western cultures is the Western emphasis of the "why/because" approach to most things and the Chinese emphasis on the "what" approach.

The second and sometimes the first questions that Westerners, especially Americans, ask in virtually all situations is "why"—and they expect an immediate "because" answer.

In China, on the other hand, over the course of some three thousand years virtually all "why/because" questions and responses were answered, and until the beginning of the modern era in China were so obvious they no longer had to be asked.

In addition, from 1644 to 1911 the Imperial government followed a policy of revering the past and maintaining the status quo. Innovation and inventions were virtually prohibited, so almost nothing changed. There was no need to ask what or seek explanations.

However, all of this changed with the opening of China to the West—which really didn't begin to happen until the late 1970s. From that period on so many new things and new ideas were introduced into China that the typical Chinese response to anything new was "what"—what is that; what are you talking about; what are you doing; what is it you want, etc.

This cultural reaction, which is still common, makes it necessary for Westerners proposing anything new to their Chinese counterparts to go into a detailed "why" explanation of whatever it is they are proposing. Often, however, what is obvious to Westerners may not be well understood by the Chinese because they are not thinking on the same channels and have not had the same experiences.

The point is that Westerners should not automatically assume that the reasons for their positions or proposals will be understood and accepted by their Chinese counterparts, so no explanations are necessary. In most cases, Westerners would be far better off to make detailed "why" explanations an integral part of their initial proposals.

DISCUSSION TOPICS & QUESTIONS

Dealing with the New China

1. With the rapid growth of capitalism and consumerism in China since 1976 and the fundamental changes this is bringing about in the Chinese mindset, the Chinese concept of "what" is gradually being forced to merge with the Western concept of "why/because."

2. This change in the Chinese way of thinking is obviously the source of most of the energy and ambitions that now drive the typical Chinese, and since there are over one billion of them their combined wants and efforts are having a direct and fundamental economic and political impact on the rest of the world.

3. Describe what you think the impact of this phenomenon could be—and very likely will be—on the world at large in 25 years; in 50 years.

4. What are some of the things you believe the U.S. and other countries could do and should do in an effort to help ensure that this new Chinese role is constructive and compatible with the rights, needs, and wants of the rest of the people in the world?

The Imperative of Self-Sufficiency

One of the most important elements in Chinese culture is an overwhelming desire—often bordering on an obsession—to be self-sufficient—on an individual, family, company, and national basis.

The reason for this culturally induced imperative is, of course, historical. Until the last two decades of the 20th century the overwhelming majority of all Chinese lived on or close to a basic subsistence level. Over the millennia millions of people died from starvation.

During these thousands of years there were a variety of village and group cooperatives created to help people sustain their livelihood, but these often failed. There were no government programs that were sufficient to prevent or remedy these disasters. There were no international aid programs when national calamities struck.

This resulted in the concept of self-sufficiency becoming an integral part of the mindset of the Chinese—an element in Chinese thinking that continues to drive individuals as well as companies, resulting in them behaving in ways that often seem to be counter-productive, or at least contrary, to others.

Many decisions made by the various agencies of the Chinese government, including the military forces, are specifically designed to enhance their self-sufficiency. Most decisions made by company managers also have a strong self-sufficiency element in them.

One of the more conspicuous demonstrations of this drive is demands by companies and government agencies that foreign countries and foreign companies wanting to do business in China agree to make their technology available to their Chinese partners.

The success of the Chinese government and individual Chinese companies in this approach to international relations is obvious, and will no doubt continue until their level of technology equals that of the world at large.

Technology-based foreign companies wanting to enter China generally must make a decision up front on how much of their technology they are willing to give their Chinese partners.

DISCUSSION TOPICS & QUESTIONS

What the Chinese Want
1. Until the last few years of the 20th century the overwhelming majority of the Chinese had little or no opportunity to change

their lifestyle, to better their lives, to fulfill many of the most basic desires and dreams that are common in humanity.

2. When the political shackles that had held most Chinese back for millennia were finally released in the late 1970s the latent energy and ambitions of millions of Chinese virtually exploded, creating a frenzy of activity that has not yet reached its zenith.

3. The primary reason underlying this amazing explosion of energy on every level of life in China was their hunger for self-sufficiency—to be independent as individuals as well as a nation.

4. How far do you think the United States and other advanced countries should go—politically and economically—to help shape the efforts of the Chinese to realize their unfettered ambitions?

5. How would you change the present China policies of the U.S. and other countries?

The Role of Formality

Despite the dramatic Westernization of the face of China and the behavior of a large and growing number of individual Chinese, the Chinese remain more formal, more structured, in their behavior than most Americans—and in that respect are much more like Europeans and Hispanics.

Businesspeople and others who visit China for the first time may get a false impression of present-day Chinese culture if they meet and interface informally with Chinese who have become Americanized and therefore behave in a non-typical way when they interact with foreigners.

It is generally safe to respond in a like manner when you are among these individuals, especially in informal situations, but when in formal situations of whatever kind one should be more formal in both speech and behavior, following the advice or lead of Chinese or experienced foreigners in how to behave.

DISCUSSION TOPICS & QUESTIONS

The American Way vs. the World

1. Generally speaking, Americans are the least formal people on Earth, and in part this is one of the reasons why other people have difficulty believing in their sincerity and goodwill. To most other people, Americans are just too casual in behavior and too quick to decide on important issues.

2. This is especially true among people, like the Chinese, whose cultures are conspicuously formal.

3. Most Americans automatically assume that their informality is both impressive and pleasing to foreigners, and instead of attempting to follow the customs of the foreign countries they are in, they too often assume that the foreigners will not be put off by their behavior.

4. Do you agree that before Americans go to China they should do all they can to learn the finer points of the formal behavior of that country?

The Food Mystique

Chinese cuisine may be the oldest cuisine in the world—and it is surely the most diverse in its ingredients. There are eight famous genres of Chinese cuisine: Anhui, Fujian, Guangdong, Hunan, Jiangsu, Shangdon, Sichuan, and Zhejiang—all of which are related to the climate, geography, and traditional agriculture of the areas concerned.

But until the 1980s getting enough food to survive had been a major aspect of Chinese life since ancient times, resulted in the famous saying, "Food is Heaven!"

This historical scarcity of food led the Chinese to spend a great deal of time thinking about it and creating images of it that went well above its normal role in life.

Over the centuries various specialty dishes in all of the regional cuisines became famous and are still well known today. This fame was based on both the ingredients and the cooking method—and finally on the names given to the dishes.

Here are some examples of these names: *Powdered Gold and Minced Jade* (sliced fish mixed with orange pieces); *Mother and Children Get Together* (quail and quail eggs cooked together); *Palm Controls the Land* (chicken cooked with bear paws); *Leaves of Wind, Frost, and Snow* (shrimp, sliced bamboo shoots, and mushrooms); *Butterflies Swarm the Peonies* (sea cucumber, prawns, chicken breast, white fungus, and water chestnuts); and, *Xiang Yu the Conqueror Says Goodbye to His Concubine* (chicken and soft-shelled turtle).

Other names for dishes referred to the four seasons, wind, flowers, snow, gold, jade, gems, animals, the moon, and colors—all designed to create a special image for the dish concerned and appeal to the sentiments of diners. Many dish names referred to famous people of the past, and had powerful historical connections.

The most popular colors used in the naming of dishes were red, yellow, white, and green—and of which are said to stimulate the appetite (while blue and azure colors are said to suppress the appetite). In keeping with the earthy appetites of the Chinese, some of the popular names for dishes are on the vulgar side.

These unusual cultural elements attached to Chinese food have helped create and sustain a mystique that remains dear to the hearts of the Chinese, linking them with their past and to each other.

Like everything else in the Chinese world, the different food ingredients are viewed as either yin or yang (positive or negative in their influence), resulting in dishes being served in a strict order that is designed to avoid unbalancing these influences.

This unwritten but deeply ingrained rule means that two yin dishes or two yang dishes should not be eaten consecutively; that they should be alternated in order to maintain the proper energy balance in the body.

DISCUSSION TOPICS & QUESTIONS

Are the Chinese on to Something?

1. The Chinese have traditionally looked upon food as something far more than just sustenance. They have also regarded it as a cultural experience that is essential for their wellbeing.

2. This concept of food appears to be generally true in most other countries—with the United States being a conspicuous exception.

3. Do you agree with the Chinese that the food one eats and the order in which it is eaten have far more meaning than just satisfying hunger and providing the necessary nutrients?

The Chinese Banquet Tradition

The one Chinese cultural tradition that virtually all foreigners know something about—and themselves enjoy—is the Chinese style banquet—the famous *yanhui* (yahn-whay) in Chinese terms. As noted above, there is an old saying in Chinese that "Food is Heaven"—an ancient reference to the fact that until the last decades of the 20th century starvation was often endemic in the country, and even in the best of times the huge mass of common Chinese subsisted on very simple fare in limited quantities.

But even the poorest of the Chinese went as far as they could during festivals on other special occasions such as weddings to indulge themselves in *yanhui.*

Virtually every special occasion in China revolves around or includes a banquet, from state dinners for visiting dignitaries and foreign businesspeople to welcoming other foreign guests, weddings, other celebrations, to family get-togethers.

Old China hands say there are invariably two characteristics of Chinese banquets—one, people eat a lot more than they ordinarily do, and two, they dine on a variety of foods that are only rarely if ever served on other occasions.

Routine *yanhui* are generally festive occasions with lots of loud talk, exaggerated actions, and speeches to honor one or more attendees. Business banquets are often marked with friendly pulling and pushing to make sure main guests are seated in a place of honor. More informal banquets often entail a lot of wrestling over the bill, as each side attempts to get one up on the other with a conspicuous show of hospitality.

Seating arrangements at formal banquets are based on the rank or status of the individual attendees. The ranking or primary guest is invariably seated on the right side of the host.

The more formal the banquet the more solicitous the host and his or her minions are in taking care of guests. Important guests at important banquets are often welcomed with a round of applause. If you get applauded, the proper response is to applaud back. At such banquets, the host normally gives the signal to start eating.

One important thing for newcomers to a Chinese banquet to keep in mind is that the various dishes are served individually over a period of time, so it isn't wise to stuff yourself on the first two or three courses. Somewhere between eight and sixteen other dishes will be served, including those that are the most important.

Toasting is a part of the banquet ritual, with *maolai* (mou-tie) being the favorite drink at large, formal events. The national toast is *gan bei* (gahn bay), which literally means "empty glass" and is the equivalent of "bottoms up."

Toasting can go on for some time, with different people taking the lead.

Guests are also generally pressured to drink, with various individuals insisting on refilling their glasses. The reason for this is not only to demonstrate extraordinary hospitality but also because it is long been the practice of Chinese hosts (along with Japanese and Korean hosts) to get their guests drunk in order to see how they behave when they are not obeying strict rules of etiquette.

Businesspeople who are treated to formal banquets one or two days after their arrival by their Chinese hosts or contacts are generally expected to reciprocate a night or two before their departure, especially if their meetings have been successful.

Notables, particularly on a state or national level, who are honored by a banquet are expected to reciprocate on their own home ground when their Chinese counterparts visit them.

DISCUSSION TOPICS & QUESTIONS

The Cultural Role of the Chinese Banquet

1. All people everywhere are generally familiar with the cultural role played by banquet style meals, but few people attach as much importance to them as the Chinese, Japanese, Koreans, and other Asians.

2. One of the most effective ways to establish close bonds with Chinese and other Asians is to know a lot about their banquet rituals, show genuine appreciation for them, and yourself host such gatherings on their behalf.

3. What banquet rituals are practiced in your own country? Have you mastered the skills of staging them? Would you feel comfortable hosting a banquet for a visiting Chinese guest?

The Ongoing Role of Festivals in China

In China, as in all older societies, festivals are one of the key links that help people keep their traditional culture alive and sustain their sense of community. Festivals are among the most conspicuous of China's cultural traditions that have survived into modern times, and the farther one gets away from the highly advanced eastern seaboard of the country the more meaningful the festivals are to the people.

There are three broad categories of festivals in China: national festivals, local-regional ethnic festivals, and tourism festivals that are usually local or regional. As the name indicates, national festivals have long histories and are generally celebrated throughout the country. Ethnic festivals also have been celebrated since ancient times and are both the most authentic and culturally the most meaningful.

Tourism festivals, as the name suggests, are mostly local festivals that are specifically aimed at attracting tourists—both domestic and foreign—and are supported by the national and local governments. Altogether there are hundreds of ethnic festivals in rural areas throughout the country, particularly in villages, towns, and cities of the ethnic minorities.

The older the festivals the more likely they are to follow the ancient lunar calendar. Some others, especially those that are primarily tourism development events, follow the Western calendar.

For the younger generations in the great cities the festivals are popular as holidays and as entertainment but the deep cultural implications they once had have faded away—and the trend is obviously continuing in the industrialized areas of China.

However, the ethnic festivals among China's minority groups in the outlying regions of the country continue to play significant roles in the beliefs and behavior of the people and will no doubt continue unabated for the foreseeable future.

All of China's festivals are, of course, reflections of the traditional culture, and they offer visitors a rare opportunity to see and experience aspects of a way of life that is thousands of years old. The ethnic festivals in particularly also serves to maintain the bonds the Chinese have with their past.

China's Three Most Important Festivals

The three most important festivals in China are the Spring Festival (*Chun Jie*/chuun jay)—China's equivalent of the West's New Years—the Dragon Boat Festival (*Duanwu Jie*/dwahn-woo jay), and the Mid-Autumn Festival (*Zhōngqui Jie*/johhg-chay jay).

The date of the month-long Spring Festival is determined by the lunar calendar, which according to the Western calendar is between the middle of January and the middle of February.

Millions of people visit their ancestral homes, families, and friends during the final days of the festival, clogging highways with cars, filling trains well beyond their rated capacity, and swamping airlines. Visitors planning on being in China during this period should prepare well in advance—and take heed of the weather, which can further exacerbate the crowding.

The event includes cleaning and decorating homes to keep evil spirits out and invite good luck in, the preparation of special foods, including sweets for the Kitchen God.

The climax of the celebration begins with New Year's Eve, which is marked by sumptuous banquets, fireworks (*bianpao*/be-in-pow), money-gifts for children, and more fireworks at midnight. New Year's Day is ushered in by more fireworks (believed to ward off evil spirits and venerate benevolent spirits), other special foods, phone calls and visits to the homes of relatives and friends.

Visitors customarily present red envelopes containing money to the families they visit, and in turn the families give money envelopes and clothing gifts to visiting children. The highlight of the day in most villages and towns is the arrival of roving bands of musicians, which pause briefly at each door to announce the arrival of spring.

The Dragon Boat Race

This festival is said to have evolved from an incident that occurred in 295 B.C., in which a famous scholar-statesman who served as an advisor to the king became the victim of a smear campaign, was discharged by the king, and subsequently jumped into a nearby river to drown himself.

His friends and spectators who witnessed the scene launched a number of boats and began racing about trying, unsuccessfully, to save him. This tragic story is credited with giving birth to the annual dragon boat race—which is featured on national and international television and therefore familiar to many Westerners.

Each boat in the race is decorated with the head and tail of a dragon, an important symbol in Chinese mythology which has traditionally been associated with kings and emperors and was believed to have dominion over water and rainfall. A drummer on each boat beats out a steady rhythm for the rowers to follow.

On the day of the festival people hang aromatic plants in their homes that are believed to ward off diseases, prepare and eat foods flavored with the essence of the plants as a digestive aid, and in some parts of China children wear embroidered amulets containing spices.

Families and friends typically eat out as part of this celebration, with *zong zi* (johng-jee), or glutinous rice wrapped in bamboo leaves, a traditional dish. The celebration takes place in early June.

The Mid-Autumn Festival

This festival, in the early fall (around September 11) when the moon is full and at its brightest, is best described as China's Family & Friend Reunion Day, for this is the occasion when Chinese families and friends traditionally come together in celebration.

This event is also marked by sumptuous outdoor feasts (where the moon can be seen and admired) at which China's famous moon cakes (baked pastries) are a featured dish. Ingredients in the cakes range from lotus seed paste, red bean paste, mixed nuts, to ham and salted egg yolk.

Double Ninth Day

Double Ninth Day (*Chongyang Jie*/chohng-yahng jee-eh) falls on the ninth day of the ninth lunar month. According to Chinese belief, the number nine is representative of the positive element in the yin-yang concept, resulting in the celebration being referred to as Chung Yang or "Double Yang" Festival.

Nine also suggests the term for longevity—something that is highly desirable. (In Taiwan Double Ninth Day is also celebrated as Senior Citizen's Day and is associated with respecting and caring for the aged.) On the Western calendar this festival is around October 9.

The Lantern Festival

The Lantern Festival (*Yuanxiao Jie*/yuu-winn-shah-oh jee-eh) is the last of the annual festivals just before the end of the year by Chinese reckoning. This ancient village celebration, sometimes referred to as a carnival, grew out of the belief that spirits could be seen flying around the first full moon of the lunar calendar.

The festival has long been marked by the display of lanterns, dancing in the streets in dragon, lion, and other costumes, and young men walking on high stilts. As usual, banquets are an important part of the festivities.

This celebration is also known as China's Valentine's Day because in earlier times this was the only day of the year that young women were allowed to leave their family compounds to view the parades as well as see young men.

There are numerous other local festivals throughout China, most of which go back for two or more thousand years. The dates of all of these events have traditionally been set by the lunar calendar, with the starting days changing from year to year. Now, many of the larger events are scheduled according to the Western calendar to accommodate foreign visitors as well as Chinese whose work and vacation schedules follow the Western calendar.

The Chinese Lunar Calendar

The traditional Chinese calendar is a lunar-solar calendar, incorporating elements of a lunar calendar with those of a solar (Western) calendar. The Western calendar is used for most day-to-day activities, but the ancient lunar calendar is still used for marking traditional Chinese holidays and in the practice of astrology.

The lunar calendar remains culturally important because it is used to designate the beginning of the country's most important festivals. The calendar is also still used in more traditional Chinese households to pick "lucky dates" for important events such as weddings, funerals, and business deals.

A special calendar, called *Huang Li* (Whahng Lee), literally "Imperial Calendar," which contains auspicious activities, times, and directions for each day, is used for this purpose. The calendar follows the Western dates along with corresponding Chinese dates that include a list of astrological measurements and elements pertaining to lucky and unlucky days. The cultural significance of the lunar calendar suggests that it will continue to be used for the foreseeable future.

The Chinese lunar calendar, said to have been created by Emperor Ti Huang in 2637 B.C., is the longest chronological record in history. It is based on exact astronomical observations of the longitude of the sun and the phases of the moon.

Because it is based on the cycles of the moon the lunar New Year can start anywhere between late January and the middle of February. A complete lunar calendar cycle takes 60 years, and is divided into five cycles of 12 years each.

Because in earlier times most Chinese were illiterate each of the 12 years of the lunar calendar was eventually named after an animal that everyone could recognize and remember. According to legend, Lord Buddha summoned all animals to come to him before his death, but only 12 showed up to bid him farewell so he rewarded them by naming the years after them in the order in which they arrived.

Most Chinese eventually came to believe that their personalities and lives were influenced by the character of the animal representing their birth year.

The 12 animals, in the order in which they arrived: rat, ox, tiger, rabbit, dragon, snake, horse, sheep, monkey, rooster, dog, and boar.

The 12-year cycle begins with an even number as the Year of the Rat—2008 for example. 2009 is therefore the Year of the Ox; 2010 the Year of the Tiger; 2011 the Year of the Rabbit; 2012 the Year of the Dragon; 2013 the Year of the Snake; and so on. 2024 becomes the next Year of the Rat; 2025 becomes the next Year of the Ox, etc.

DISCUSSION TOPICS & QUESTIONS

When in Rome...

1. One of the most pleasant and most effective ways to experience foreign cultures is to learn about their traditional festivals and to participate in them when that is allowed.

2. This is also one of the most effective ways for demonstrating your respect for the culture of others and to establish bonds with them.

3. Have you ever participated in festival in a foreign country? And if not, why not?

Birthdays & Weddings

Until modern times the Chinese were regarded as one year old on the day they were born. All Chinese became two years old on the first New Year's after their birth. Nowadays, virtually all Chinese count their age from the date of their birth, as in Western countries.

Traditionally, Chinese families did not celebrate the birth of babies until they were one month old—because so many of them died before reaching that age—and more traditional families have continued that tradition.

On this occasion the parents of newborn babies both give and receive gifts from relatives and friends. These gifts vary with the region but they invariably include eggs that have been dyed red—the shape of the eggs representing harmony and happiness, and the color signifying happiness.

Other gifts received by the parents include a variety of food items, supplies and apparel for the babies, and red envelopes containing money. In earlier times grandparents did their best to give silver or gold (always more trustworthy than paper money). Whatever the gifts, they are always given in even numbers to ward off bad luck. The final event of the day is a feast at home or at a restaurant, hosted by the new parents. This custom is still followed by most Chinese.

A child's second birthday has also long been an auspicious event in China—and one of the customs on this occasion has been to sit the toddler in the middle of the floor and surround it with books, coins, dolls and so on to see which one it picks up first. The belief was that children who pick up coins may become rich; those who pick up books may become teachers; and those who reach for dolls may have many children.

Most urban Chinese families now follow birthday practices that are similar to those in the West, but with special attention paid to certain ages. The 60th, 70th, 80th, and 90th birthdays are especially celebrated, with gifts and banquet parties. Foods that are symbolic of health and prosperity (eggs) and longevity (long noodles) are invariably served on these occasions.

Baby boys continue to be preferred over girls because that helps ensure the continued existence of the ancestral family line.

Weddings

Formal marriages have been customary in China for some three thousand years, and in upper classes have been very intricate affairs with an extensive protocol because of the importance of maintaining the family names, many of which date back to the founding clan leaders.

All marriages were arranged, and the higher the class of the family the more elaborate the original contacts and arrangements prior to the weddings themselves. (See Part III for present-day marriage customs.)

Myths & Superstitions in China

Myths and superstitions have played a vital role in the lives of the Chinese since ancient times, and still today superstitions play an important role in the culture. There are superstitions about colors, dates, certain numbers, certain foods, about flowers and plants, about housecleaning, about paying all debts before the end of the year, and so on.

There are numerous superstitions pertaining to activity on New Year's Day because it is believed that things done on that day set the stage for what may come during the rest of the year. Crying, cursing, getting angry, washing your hair, etc., on New Year's Day are taboo. Red is a happy, good luck color. The sound of firecrackers chase away evil spirits.

In earlier times there were, in fact, so many superstitions in China that somebody in more traditional families was responsible for keeping track of them. They were also listed in various manuals and other literature. You can now find numerous references on the Internet—but a growing number of Chinese ignore the vast majority of them.

One of the more interesting myths—that is symbolically represented today throughout China in various signs and festivals—is that the Chinese are the descendants of dragons.

Probably the best-known Chinese superstition today has to do with numbers. Most even numbers are considered lucky, with "eight" and its combinations (88, 888, up to 88,888,888) being the most valued of all because the Chinese word for eight, $b\bar{o}$ (bah), also has the meaning of "fortune." Four (si/she), on the other hand, is regarded as a bad luck word because it is also the word for "death."

Two odd numbers, five ($w\bar{o}$/woo) and nine ($ji\bar{o}$/jew) are also especially favored, with "five" playing a more important role in Chinese culture than "eight"—the five elements of Chinese cosmology (metal, wood, water, fire, and earth); the five tastes (sweet, sour, salty, bitter, and pungent); the five basic colors (red, green, yellow, black, and white); and the ideal family (three boys and two girls).

Both eights and fives continue to play key roles in the lives of the Chinese, from addresses, license numbers, choice of office and apartment floors, gifts, to the ideal number of guests at banquets.

DISCUSSION TOPICS & QUESTIONS

Dealing with Superstitions

1. What are some of the possible business and personal ramifications in not being able to deal effectively with the deeply embedded superstitions of China?

2. What would you say are the cultural origins of some of the most common superstitions in China?

3. Would you agree that some of the so-called superstitions of China have either a valid scientific or psychological basis?

The Feng-Shui Factor

One of the more fascinating aspects of China's traditional culture is the practice of geomancy or divination, known in Chinese as *feng-shui* (foong shway), which literally means "wind and water," and has to do with the orientation of buildings, doors, furniture, and other manmade things of a semi-permanent nature.

The Chinese have traditionally believed that the orientation of such things in relation to the points of the compass, nearby hills, bodies of water, forests, etc., has a profound influence, either negative or positive, on the fortunes of people by increasing or diminishing the flow of *qi* (chee) or energy that is manifested by these things.

According to this Chinese concept, buildings, doors, and other things that are oriented in such a way that they block the natural flow of *qi* have a negative impact on the lives of the people using them, and they go to great pains—of often considerable expense—to make sure that the dictates of *feng-shui* are met in the orientation and design of buildings and in the placement of doors and furniture, etc.

Feng-shui is based on the Chinese belief that all things in nature are inter-related, and that things and people must reflect the balance of nature in order to be in harmony with the energy reflected by them. Achieving this balance is believed to be directly related to one's health and success in life.

There are recorded examples in Hong Kong (for example) of the occupants of foreign-designed buildings having nothing but bad luck until they called in a *feng-shui* expert and accepted his or her advice on remodeling or completely redoing the building from scratch—following which their luck changed for the better.

Geomancy has been known and used in the Western world, particularly in Egypt and among the Indian tribes of Mexico and Peru, since ancient times, but in most of the West it has been virtually ignored and dismissed as primitive nonsense—and this despite the fact that everyone, automatically, intuitively, has an opinion about how things should be oriented.

All of the West's better architects and interior designers practice the art of *feng-shui* without necessarily referring to it by this name or as geomancy (in order not to frighten clients!)—and even the term *feng-shui* itself is gradually being accepted in the world language.

Traditionally, Chinese geomancy practitioners used a Luopan compass—originally a scientific instrument used in making astronomical observations to synchronize the solar and lunar calendars—to decide precisely how to orient buildings and other things.

Luopan compasses are for sale today specifically for use by geomancers, but those who are well experienced in the art can do without it—using their well-honed inner feelings to confirm what they see in the immediate surroundings.

A growing number of Western scientists and people in generally have begun to agree that the Chinese have been correct all along, and that all life and all things in the cosmos are inter-related and that *qi* actually exists—and that *feng-shui* makes sense.

DISCUSSION TOPICS & QUESTIONS

What the West Can Learn from China

1. There are a number of elements in China's traditional culture, from acupuncture to *tai qi quwan* (their traditional form of exercising), that are gradually being accepted by Westerners as having significant merit, and are increasingly being adopted by a growing number of people.

2. The Chinese have long understood that the body and mind are interrelated and mutually dependent, and many aspects of their traditional culture have reflected this understanding. In the Western world, on the other hand, religious beliefs have traditionally viewed the body and mind as separate entities— often causing great harm to both.

3. Do you believe that there are, in fact, fundamental things about life and the cosmos that Westerners can learn from China?

China's Martial Arts Legacy

Historically, most cultures of any size developed a number of indigenous martial arts as a matter of self-defense and survival because there has always been a predatory element in the make-up of human beings.

Given the turbulence of China's 5,000-year history it is not surprising that the Chinese have the longest sustained heritage of martial arts of any country in the world, but what is surprising is the influence some of these arts now have on millions of people, young and old, around the world today.

Chinese martial arts, *wushu* (woo-shuu) in Chinese, included all of the well-known weapons such as bows and arrows, spears, swords, and the like, but what is virtually unique in the contribution the Chinese have made to martial arts is the art of defensive and offensive fighting without weapons, using only the bare hands and feet.

What is also remarkable is that for the most part the martial arts that are known and practiced around the world today were not originally created or promoted by professional soldiers. They were the creation of Buddhist priests.

The reason for this is simple. Throughout most of China's history priests and other common people were not allowed to own or carry weapons of any kind, and therefore had no effective way to defend themselves.

Ordinary people, including priests, were especially susceptible to being attacked by brigands when they traveled about the country, and as the generations passed various schools of martial arts appeared and flourished.

Being well-educated in the classic philosophies of China, and also being keen observers of nature, priests brought a special dimension to the forms of fighting they developed, integrating tactics they learned from snakes, tigers, and other animals.

Instead of relying on brawn in their defensive and offensive measures these extraordinary people emphasized use of the brain to defend themselves and defeat attackers. These measures including identifying all of the points on the body that are especially susceptible to trauma when hit by a relatively modest force, and how to turn the strength and fighting forms of their opponents against them.

As time passed, the methods taught and used by the priests of the Shaolin Monastery in *Zhengzhou* (Henan Province) became the most famous of the many martial arts schools in China, at least among foreign advocates. And now the martial arts of the Shaolin Temple, usually referred to as *kung fu*, are the ones that foreigners are most likely to hear about.

Wushu refers to martial arts in a more general sense, while *kung fu* applies more to the style that has become famous internationally as a result of movies, television shows, comics, and various sports media.

Today *kung fu* is not taught or practiced just as a way of fighting. It is regarded and taught as an aesthetic practice, as a philosophical experience involving the integration of the mind and the body with the cosmos, as a way of exercising both the body and mind to improve one's mental outlook and health, to develop discipline, and to raise moral standards, particularly emphasizing good manners and good conduct in general.

The Shaolin Temple now sponsors two martial arts festivals annually, especially aimed at members of the World International Wushu Federation, that attract a growing number of people from around the world.

An increasing number of foreign martial arts devotees can be found in China throughout the year, studying with *wushu* masters. This will no doubt help spread the knowledge around the world that China—not Japan—gave birth to most of Asia's martial arts traditions.

DISCUSSION TOPICS & QUESTIONS

Martial Arts as a Cultural Medium

1. Philosophers as well as military men the world over have known since ancient times that martial arts training has a profound influence on the character and overall mindset and behavior

of people, but until recent times training in martial arts was designed to enhance combat skills for military purposes.

2. Following the end of the samurai and shogunate era in Japan in the late 1860s, Japanese masters of judo, kendo, and karate transformed these ancient fighting arts into sports aimed at instilling the most desirable traits into people—from honesty, truthfulness, ambition, and courage to perseverance in pursuing goals. In the late 1900s Chinese masters of kungfu and other traditional martial arts followed the Japanese example and began teaching them as character-building sports.

3. Do you think it would be wise to make the teaching of a martial art—karate or kendo, for example—mandatory in all elementary and high schools around the world?

China's Theatrical Traditions

There are said to be 368 forms of *daxi* (dah-she) or opera in China, the best known of which is Beijing Opera. The origin of opera in China is unknown, but there are copious records and references to this form of entertainment going back well over two thousand years.

The action in Chinese operas is based on strong movements representing a variety of actions, from riding a horse, rowing a boat, to engaging in battle. Dialogue includes recitations, speeches, and singing. Characters are clearly defined by their attire and makeup. Traditional string and percussion instruments provide the musical background for the action.

Beijing opera actors can chose from over one thousand plays, most of them drawn from historical novels that have political and military themes.

During the communist revolution of the 1930s and 40s cultural troupes were assigned to the Red Army, with the goal of promoting communist ideology within the army as well as among the general population in the areas the armies controlled.

Following the takeover of China by the communist party in 1949 the use of opera as a political tool was continued. At the same time, the government encouraged the development of new operas with historical and modern themes.

But during the Cultural Revolution (1966-1976) most opera troupes were disbanded, and performers as well as scriptwriters were severely persecuted. The only exception to this were eight operas touting the communist ideology that were approved by Jiang Qing, a consort of Chairman Mao, and her so-called "Gang of Four"—who became more and more powerful as Mao became weak from age and various illnesses.

Following the downfall of the Gang of Four and Mao's death the tradition of opera was revived, with new plays and new theaters proliferating. The advent of television provided a popular new media for operatic productions. Today, modern and classic operas are one of China's greatest cultural treasures, and are something that foreign visitors should not miss.

Virtually every city in China has one or more opera theaters that play an important role in the cultural life of the people. Plays presented in these theaters generally have their own local or regional themes that are usually historical—making them both entertaining and educational.

Visitors to China should make a point of attending a number of operas to get a deep and abiding feel for the essence and nuance of Chinese culture.

DISCUSSION TOPICS & QUESTIONS

Using Art as a Political Tool

1. The Chinese government continues to use the theater as a medium for spreading political messages, mostly propaganda. Do you think this method of influencing the public is effective, and do you approve of it?

2. Does your government use the theater for political purposes?

The Art of Puppetry

Puppetry is another classic form of entertainment in China that goes back for thousands of years, and is something that visitors should be aware of—and experience while they are in China.

There are a variety of puppet forms, all of which are highly advanced technologically speaking, with master puppeteers who seemingly bring them to life.

One promotional piece announcing a coming "rod puppet" performance promised that the puppets and their skilled handlers would present an acrobatic spectacular that all of the family would enjoy, with incredible stunts, including: "face changing, flinging the rosary, writing with a brush and painting. Traditional dance and drama will also be included in the show."

Among the most popular of the puppet programs are: The Lion Dance, Wu Song Killing the Tiger, The Crane and the Tortoise, The Fat Man and the Mosquito, The Fan Dance, Ping Pong Diplomacy, The Lady in the Moon, Acrobatics Skills: The Cyclists, The Dance of the Flower Fairies, The Monkey King Thrice Beats the Bony Ghost, The Ancient Art of Puppetry, and The Dragon Dance. The Dragon Dance is regarded as one of the finest demonstrations of folk arts in China. It is performed to the tune of Chinese folk percussion and wind instruments and string music typical of the Yangzhou region. The "dragons" perform all the movements of a life-size dragon dance: they roll over, cross over and under their serpentine bodies, form into a circle, and play with a ball. The Yangzhou Puppet Theatre is described as the largest and most famous puppet troupe in China. It is also described as being characterized by vividness and refinement, with the puppeteers able to inject life into the puppets to make them impressively lifelike.

This is another category of Chinese culture that is both entertaining and educational, and is highly recommended for foreign residents and visitors alike.

The Cultural Role of Calligraphy In Chinese Culture

In ancient times only the relatively affluent and elite members of Chinese society were able to study the reading and drawing of the

Hanzi. As time passed, adding an artistic quality to the individual drawings took on a role and importance of its own, eventually reaching the point where the drawings of those who were especially skillful achieved the level of a fine art.

Given the focus of the ancient Chinese on both art and quality it wasn't long before the artistry of one's drawings came to be regarded as a measure of his cultural achievement, his personality, and his worth as a human being. This led to the emergence of *shufa* (shuu-fahh), or calligraphy, as one of the most esteemed artistic and culture achievements in Chinese society.

Examples of the finest *shufa* became treasured objects that were sought after by the well-to-do and displayed as fine art in homes, offices, and museums. The cultural tradition of *shufa* was passed on to Korea and Japan, where it often played an even more important role in the cultural life of the people. Still today in Japan all traditionally styled homes and inns have special alcoves (*tokonoma*/toe-koe-no-mah) where examples of calligraphy are displayed.

Examples of Chinese *shufa*, both classic and modern, are sold in art and gift shops as framed interior decorative scrolls. Classic examples in particular are wonderful representations of China's superb arts and crafts, with mountain scenes among the most popular.

Western admirers of Chinese art have been buying *shufa* for more than two hundred years.

Foreign students of the Chinese language are also urged to include learning how to draw the characters in their studies because they convey powerful cultural meanings.

DISCUSSION TOPICS & QUESTIONS

The Importance of Handwriting Skills

1. In earlier times in the Western world, as in China and elsewhere in Asia, the quality of one's handwriting was equated with the level of education and cultural achievement, and cal-

ligraphy was practiced as an art form. Both the quality of hand-writing and the practice of calligraphy have diminished significantly in the West, but they remain prized arts in China.

2. Would you advocate that Western countries emulate China in maintaining high standards for hand-writing as an important element in their cultures? Explain your rationale.

Literature in Chinese Culture

Literature has probably played a more important role in the history and cultural life of China than in any other country. By the 6th century B.C. historians, biographers, poets, and songwriters were flourishing and having a major, direct impact on the lives of the educated class, and a powerful indirect influence on the lives of the uneducated, including peasants.

The quality of the prose and poetry produced during this period rivals anything that was to come much later in the Western world. This was the millennium that give birth to the great scholar-philosopher-writers, Tzu, Confucius, Mencius, and many lesser lights who enriched the culture of the country and whose influence is still felt today in modern China. An anthology produced during the Tang Dynasty (618-907 A.D.) contains 50,000 poems.

Foreign residents and visitors to China would be well advised to familiarize themselves with some of the classics of Chinese literature. Not only will it give them a better appreciation of the legacy of Chinese culture, it will help them make friends and influence people.

Present-day historians and scholars say that the most notable achievement of Yuan Dynasty (1280-1368 A.D.) literature was *zaju* (jah-juu), or poetic dramas set to music. *Snow in Midsummer* by celebrated playwright Guan Hanqing and *The Western Chamber* written by another *zaju* master, Wang Shipu, are regarded as masterpieces of this ancient form of drama.

Novels written during the Ming (1368-1644 A.D.) and Qing (1644-1911 A.D.) dynasties are still popular sellers in China. These include the four masterpieces *The Three Kingdoms* by Luo Guan-zhong, *Outlaws of the Marsh* by Shi Nai'an, *Journey to the West* by Wu Cheng'en, and *A Dream of Red Mansions* by Cao Xueqin. They have been celebrated for centuries for their rich historical and cultural insights and unique style.

Most educated Chinese today know the names and the work of many of the greatest of these ancient playwrights, poets, and writers—and they respond quickly when foreigners demonstrate similar knowledge.

Contemporary Literature

The new cultural movement that emerged in China in the 1920s was an anti-imperialist and anti-feudal movement. Progressive writers, represented by Lu Xun, gave birth to modern Chinese literature.

The most outstanding representative works of this era are the novels *The Diary of a Madman* and *The True Story of Ah Q* by Lu Xun, the poetry anthology *The Goddesses* by Guo Moruo, the novel *Midnight* by Mao Dun, the trilogy novels *Family, Spring,* and *Autumn* by Ba Jin, the novel *Camel Xiangzi* by Lao She, and the plays *Thunderstorm* and *Sunrise* by Cao Yu.

Mao Zedong, the leader of the revolution that brought the communists to power in 1949, was a prolific poet and writer. In fact, it can be said that he succeeded in this watershed event primarily *because* of his talents as a writer.

Deng Xiaoping, who succeeded Mao in 1967, was also a prolific writer, and his collected works are available in translations. But neither Mao nor Deng were exceptions in their time, and still today huge numbers of Chinese are given to writing in one form or another, with many of them specializing in political treatises. Writing has, in fact, been a cultural obsession in China since ancient times.

Chinese literature, both ancient and contemporary, serve as doorways to the culture of China, providing insights into how and why the Chinese think and behave the way they do. Both foreign residents and visitors would be well advised to add translations of Chinese literature to their reading list.

Being able to refer to the work of famous Chinese authors, modern or classic, including quoting from Confucius, Mencius, and other philosophers, and from such famous poets as *Po Li*, will gain you a lot of mileage in your Chinese relationships.

Visitors to China who are interested in the writings of Mao can readily find copies of his *Little Red Book*, containing a collection of the quotations and sayings that became the bible of his regime and the millions of young people who became "Red Guards" in the 1966-1976 Cultural Revolution. (You can also buy the book in some bookshops in other countries and from online booksellers.)

During the revolution hundreds of millions of copies of the book were sold because being caught without a copy was a serious offense. After Mao died in 1976 sales of the book dropped off to virtually nothing but by the 1990s interest in both Mao and the revolutionary period began to grow, and it is now an annual bestseller, earning millions of dollars for the government agency that owns his archives.

The name of the book in Chinese is *Mao Zhuxi Yulu* (mah-oh juu-she yuu-luu), which literally means "The Quotes of Chairman Mao."

DISCUSSION TOPICS & QUESTIONS

The Importance of Literature

1. Literature, or at least the written word, has proven to be one of the most powerful political tools in existence, and has been responsible for most of the great changes in human behavior since writing was first invented.

2. Can you name two books written by Chinese philosophers in ancient times that had a profound influence on Chinese culture as well as the cultures of Korea and Japan?

3. What single book do you think had the most influence on the young people of China during the "Cultural Revolution?" Why do you think this happened?

Religion in Today's China

Officially there are said to be some 100 million people in China who are recognized members of various "religions," including Buddhism, Confucianism, and Taoism.

All of these three belief systems have had a deep and fundamental impact on Chinese culture, but Confucianism, historically the most important of the three in practical terms, is more about sociology and politics than theology, with its primary influence being on interpersonal relationships in all areas and on all levels of society and its ultimate goal being harmony and stability in real life.

Buddhism, which is concerned with both secular and spiritual behavior, is also more philosophical than theological, and does not include the kind of absolute moral social and spiritual commandments that are the bedrock of Christianity and Islam.

Taoism is far more esoteric than Buddhism and Confucianism. Among other things it teaches that it is better to do nothing than to try and fail, and that the highest calling for humanity is to merge with the cosmos.

By Western standards (which, of course, are generally not lived up to by most people) the Chinese are not a very religious people in that they do not attend churches or mosques regularly, do not pray regularly, and do not talk about or write about their "religions" as Westerners do.

Both Buddhism and Confucianism are more concerned about real-time lifestyles than they are about people going to Heaven after they die by professing to believe in a particular god or the emissary of a god.

Most Chinese follow various Buddhist rituals in such life passages as birth, marriage, and death but these are mostly formalities that do not impact on other areas of life.

China's philosophies and so-called religions did not claim absolute exclusivity and did not attempt to convert or destroy nonbelievers so they did not result in the strife, wars, and emotional suffering that have plagued the Western and mid-Eastern world since the creation of Judaism, Christianity, and Islam.

In addition to Buddhism, Confucianism, and Taoism, there are relatively large numbers of Muslims and Christians in China, along with a number of other lesser known faiths. Despite government laws proclaiming the right of the Chinese to follow whatever religion they choose, the government maintains a list of the religions that are approved.

Religious sects that are not on the government's approved list are subject to being suppressed. There are also regulations prohibiting proselytizing by adherents of religions that are not approved

In the past, a number of Chinese who were to become prominent as political leaders became members of various Christian denominations when young and/or when they were in exile. Generally, their Christian beliefs did not replace their Buddhist and Confucian beliefs but were merely added to them.

The amazing rise in China's living standards during the 1980s and 90s had one unexpected and remarkable result—an astounding jump in the popularity of Buddhism.

By the middle of the first decade of the 21st century media reports noted that "millions" of affluent urban Chinese had suddenly gone back to following Buddhist rituals in an apparent rejection of the new materialism that was sweeping the country.

In addition to various Buddhist paraphernalia becoming best-sellers, huge numbers of people began flocking to temples on the first day of every lunar month to burn incense and "restore their sense of having a soul."

The number of people going to monasteries on retreats from "working 12 hours a day six days a week" also increased dramatically—with some of the more affluent flying to Thailand to visit famous Buddhist sites.

Generally speaking, the Chinese government does not approve of religious proselytizing of any kind by any religion, and present-day Christian missionaries who go there seeking new converts are advised to keep a very low profile.

Visitors to China are also generally advised to refrain from talking about religion to anyone outside of their close circle of friends.

DISCUSSION TOPICS & QUESTIONS

1. What do you think of the Chinese government's position on religion?

2. American and European missionaries have been active in China since the early 1800s. What do you think of this effort to spread some form of Christianity in China?

3. What aspects of Christianity do you think have been the most effective in bringing about fundamental changes in the way many ordinary Chinese think?

PART III

Chinese Culture Today

Most of the cultural changes that have already taken place in China and are continuing to occur on a daily basis, particularly in the more industrialized eastern regions of the country, can be directly traced to the importation of American business practices and social customs, including popular entertainment. But even in the remote western areas of China cultural changes are evident in many ways, from the apparel the people wear to their use of cell phones and the Internet.

The amazing bustle of activity that is continuing to change the face of China and the character of the Chinese is being fueled by an incredible outpouring of energy that one can both see and feel, and is something that makes present-day China one of the world's most exciting business and travel destinations.

Among the most conspicuous and impressive symbols of modern China is its growing profusion of Western-style buildings with extraordinary architectural features. A number of these towering structures, particularly in Shanghai, became world-class landmarks the instant they were completed.

For many visitors a building that also symbolizes the new China is the Center for the Performing Arts just off of Tiananmen Square in Beijing, within 200 yards of the mausoleum of Mao Zedong. This extraordinary oval shaped structure resembles a space ship, and houses three theaters—one for opera, one for ballet, and one for stage plays.

Beijing's huge international airport is even more symbolic of today's China. Rushed to completion in time for the 2008 Summer Olympics, this soaring dragon-like golden-roofed structure is nearly two miles long and covers 240 acres—making it both the largest airport terminal in the world as well as the world's largest covered structure.

A less visible but perhaps even more important cultural symbol of modern-day China is the American-invented debit card system—now used by millions of Chinese shoppers, especially those traveling abroad, where they have replaced the Japanese as the biggest spenders.

The operator of the Chinese debit card network, China-Union Pay Company, has some of its cards printed in Japan, where the cards are widely accepted by a variety of businesses. As of this writing, the Chinese banks providing the cards have issued 1.3 billion cards—the equivalent of the entire population of the country. This suggests China is on a cultural and economic roll with no end in sight.

DISCUSSION TOPICS & QUESTIONS

The Face of New China

1. The more the common culture of China transforms from traditional concepts and customs to a Western-style culture the more influence this will have on the mindset of top government leaders. The change has already been significant but it has a long way to go before it approaches democratic ideals.

2. Can you extrapolate on the depth of this change in government leaders over a period of time, and visualize what it will mean in terms of their political, economic and social policies?

3. What are some of the most significant advantages that China has over fully democratic societies as a result of its one-party system?

Fulfilling 5,000 Years of Suppressed Needs, Wants & Ambitions

For more than three thousand years the vast majority of all Chinese did not have the political or social freedom to make decisions on their own. They were culturally conditioned to suppress their own personal needs and ambitions and to think and behave in terms of collective responsibility—first for their families, then for their community, next for their clan, and ultimately for the nation at large.

This mindset was, in fact, the foundation of the teachings of Confucius, the greatest of all Chinese sages, and was based on the already old Chinese idea that social stability was far more important than allowing people to make decisions on their own.

Within a few generations this Confucian philosophy was adopted as the official creed of the Imperial Court and was mandated as the law of the land—an action that was to have a profound impact on the values and attitudes of Chinese that is still visible in modern-day China.

As time passed the concept and practice of collective behavior rather than personal actions became so deeply embedded in Chinese culture that individualism virtually disappeared from the society. Broadly speaking the Chinese became docile and cooperative—until they were pushed to the extremes by venal overlords, and then they would rebel.

Over the centuries the country as a whole paid a great price for the suppression of individual thought and action because that prevented the overwhelming majority of Chinese from doing anything to change their material status quo. The damage that it did to the spirit of the people can only be imagined.

Despite the rise and fall of one imperial dynasty after the other—combined with invasions by Mongolians (who conquered and ruled China from 1280 to 1368), by the Manchu (who conquered and ruled China from 1644 to 1911), and finally by the Japanese who invaded and occupied Eastern and Northern China from the 1930s to 1945—the Confucian concept of collectivism continued to be the bedrock of Chinese culture until the late 1970s.

The limitations and restrictions imposed upon the Chinese for millennia by Confucianism were lax compared to what the Communist regime of Mao Zedong imposed on the Chinese from 1949 until 1976. But Mao, a champion of women's rights, was a liberator in many ways.

DISCUSSION TOPICS & QUESTIONS

Confucianism vs. Communism

1. There are many similarities in Confucianism and in the form of Communism now practiced by Chinese leaders. What are some of these similarities?

2. What are some of the most conspicuous benefits that the Chinese people now enjoy that were banned by Confucianism?

3. What are some of the most conspicuous benefits that the Chinese people now enjoy—that did not exist before—as a result of the one-party system that is primarily based on communist ideology?

4. Why are most Chinese *not* members of the Communist Party, and why do most of those who *are* members join the Party?

The "Get Rich is Glorious" Tipping Point

The first telling blow against the rigid Confucian-based suppression of the minds and hearts of the Chinese was, in fact, struck by Mao, founder of the Communist government of China in 1949, who looked upon collective-based Confucianism as one of the primary reasons for the failure of China to keep up with the West following the Industrial Revolution.

Mao used the first eighteen years of his regime in a massive attempt to remold the Chinese into paragons of communism—something he called "The Great Leap Forward"—but the effort was a total disaster. In 1966, in desperation, he initiated a violent

"Culture Revolution" that was aimed at destroying all of the vestiges of traditional Chinese thought and behavior.

He died in 1976 and the revolution died with him, but the damage inflicted upon the Confucian-oriented culture was profound and set the stage for a second but peaceful and entirely different kind of revolution inaugurated in the early 1970s by his successor, his former but disillusioned Communist ally Deng Xiaoping. (Mao had Deng purged and exiled to the country during the Cultural Revolution.)

Recalled to Beijing by the Polit-Bureau, Deng soon proclaimed that "To get rich is glorious!" and little by little over the next decade made it possible for ordinary Chinese to utilize their long-suppressed ambitions and skills, to begin thinking and acting as individuals, and to help themselves for the first time in the long history of the country.

Future historians will no doubt see this phenomenon as one of the most auspicious events in human history, as within less than two decades it freed over one billion people from a kind of cultural and political enslavement that had often treated them more like objects rather than human beings throughout their existence.

By the early 1990s, old-timers who knew China before the beginning of the "get rich" era could only marvel—almost in disbelief—at what the Chinese had accomplished since Deng's simple announcement.

DISCUSSION TOPICS & QUESTIONS

The Energy that Grows Out of Freedom

1. The United States owes its incredible wealth and versatility to a political system that makes it possible for people to make decisions on their own, to do—within limits—what they want to do, and to be as successful as possible, given their talents, energy, and luck.

2. The astounding energy that is released by personal freedom has also been demonstrated since the 1950s by Japan, Hong Kong,

Korea, Taiwan, China, and finally Russia—who are among the most conspicuous examples.

3. Do you believe the strict political limitations imposed on the people of China by the government are justified? Explain your answer.

4. Do you believe that the restrictions on religious freedom imposed by the Chinese government have a positive or negative effect on the culture and the economy? Explain your reasoning.

"Big Brother" is Alive and Thriving

Deng Xiaoping and his cohorts were not as magnanimous in allowing the people of China to become capitalistic entrepreneurs as it might have seemed to uninformed outsiders. The government was, in fact, calculating and clever. It harnessed the ambitions and energies of the billion Chinese to serve its own purpose by reserving a huge piece of the capitalistic action for itself.

The central government of China made sure that it owned a stake in virtually every new enterprise of any size and importance in the country. Among other measures, Deng first gave the green light to start new enterprises to huge numbers of Communist Party cadres.

He also made special deals with Overseas Chinese tycoons in Hong Kong, Singapore, and elsewhere in Asia, as well as multinational American and European companies, to entice them to invest in China—with the government profiting directly and indirectly.

New would-be entrepreneurs who were not among the favored cadres pre-approved for business licenses generally found it necessary to join the Communist Party and agree to give shares of their companies to local and regional government agencies and officials.

Today the Chinese government directly and indirectly controls a significant percentage of all of the more important companies in China. The military establishment alone is said to be the largest business conglomerate in the country.

Obviously, this degree of Chinese government ownership and control has not been all bad. In fact, whether or not it was by design or by accident it brought a great deal of coherence and order to the dramatic changes that were to remake China.

The Chinese government is now actively pursuing a program to increase the amount of personal freedom individuals have, to explain itself more thoroughly to the rest of the world, and to raise the level of knowledge and appreciation of its cultural worldwide.

DISCUSSION TOPICS & QUESTIONS

The Power of Authoritarianism

1. It cannot be denied that the dictatorial control that China's leaders exercised during the first decades of the country's rise to economic prominence played a significant role in transforming China from the economic and cultural wasteland left by Mao Zedong into an economic superpower.

2. Many elements of this authoritarian control are still starkly visible in present-day China. Do you believe that the United States and other Western countries should continue to push China's leaders to adopt a fully democratic system of government?

3. What about other countries that ostensibly have democratic governments but in reality deny or subvert the rights inherent in democracy, and are democratic in name only? Should they be encouraged or forced to change?

The American Influence On Chinese Culture

As soon as the Chinese—particularly those on the Eastern Seaboard—were politically free to help themselves they began a frenzied effort to transform their way of working and living. While their motivation was very personal, it was also inspired by the visions they had of America as a land of opportunity in which anyone could become rich—an image that was strongly encouraged by the government for reasons of national interests.

By the 1990s signs of American influence were visible in much of China. One of the most extraordinary of these signs was a McDonald's Restaurant on a street bordering Beijing's famed Tiananmen Square—a place that had become the face of the new China. (It was moved a few years later.)

In fact, the remaking of the Chinese mindset required almost no time at all. The intelligence and the skills they needed to start remaking the country had always been there. They had just been locked down. With the American Way as their model they were able to achieve warp speed in no time in beginning the transformation of China both culturally and physically.

The Influence of Computers And the Internet on Chinese Culture

The appearance of computers and the Internet in China were to have an equally pervasive influence on the thinking and behavior of the Chinese—further weaning them away from the traditional culture as well as the communist culture of the Mao era.

One of the key elements in the cultural changes brought on by computers was the fact that the computer itself is culturally neutral—that is, unlike human beings it does not come with any culture hardwired into it. It is not pre-programmed to require any obedience to existing cultural norms.

Like Americans, Japanese, Koreans, and other computer users, large numbers of Chinese were freed for the first time in the history of the country to think like and act like individuals without any thought of their social status, gender, or relationships with others.

The appearance of digital video games was also to have an especially profound influence on the attitudes and behavior of young Chinese. Millions of children in families whose income had risen above subsistence levels began spending hours playing video games that had both an obvious and a subtle influence on their way of thinking and acting.

The role models in these games were not the selfless, self-sacrificing, well-mannered heroes of Confucian China. They were the individualistic, independent, self-serving, fashion-oriented, sensual-minded and acting characters embellished by the imagination and creativity of Japanese *anime* and *manga* (comic) masters.

Unintentionally, the war that Chairman Mao had begun in 1966 against the traditional mindset and behavior of the Chinese was taken one giant leap forward by the creators of these video games. By the end of 2008 the number of Internet users in China had surpassed that of all other countries in the world, and Chinese Internet companies had begun to go international, first into Japan and then into other neighboring countries.

As the use of the Internet grew in China it gave voice to millions of people who before had been mute and isolated, with few means beyond putting up posters on walls—a dangerous activity—to makes their discontent and views known. Despite the fact that the content of the Internet was and still is controlled to a considerable extent by the government, the impact it had on the ability of ordinary Chinese to make their voices heard was seminal.

One might say that computers and the Internet helped lower the Great Wall of the traditional Chinese mindset.

DISCUSSION TOPICS & QUESTIONS

The Power of Technology

1. What is the basic, fundamental element in technology that makes it possible for the most hidebound traditionalists—the people who have been so thoroughly programmed by customs, by religions, and by philosophies that they cannot think outside of these boxes—to change their behavior in a virtual instant?

2. After people change their behavior because of the power of technology, how likely are they to change their way of thinking? How likely is this change to be pro-human and constructive rather than the opposite?

3. Do you approve of China's policy of strictly controlling Internet content, even if this control is designed to prevent the technology from being used to debase their culture?

The Second Cultural Revolution

The combination of the "get rich quick" policy initiated by Mao's successor in the late 1970s and the widespread use of computers in China in the following decade resulted in a second cultural revolution—this time one that was proposed and aided by the government but was primarily the work of the people themselves—by individuals.

There was not one area or one aspect of Chinese life in the large eastern urban areas of the country that was not fundamentally changed by the economic and social revolution initiated by Deng, the new chairman of China.

Shortly after the beginning of the Deng era I engaged a taxi driver to show me some of the physical changes taking place in Beijing. During our conversations he complained bitterly that the changes were not taking place fast enough—that government agencies and ministries were stalling; that all of their top officials were more interested in helping themselves to the new spoils than in helping common people.

He bragged, however, that he earned more money than any minister in the government—a sign to me that the ancient dragon of China had stood up and was going to be heard from. Some five years after the beginning of the Deng period I read that a small group of local farmers in a distant province had chartered a plane to take them to Beijing on a shopping trip—an absolutely incredible change from the past.

DISCUSSION TOPICS & QUESTIONS

China's Next Door Neighbor

1. Given the obvious incredible advances that China made economically, socially, and politically between 1976 and 2006, why

do you think North Korea, their next door neighbor, remained stuck in a time-warp during the same period—and in many respects after 2006 continued to resemble a vast slave-labor camp?

2. Do you believe China should have been more aggressive in encouraging North Korea's leaders to understand and accept the reality dictated by simple common sense, saving ordinary North Koreans from decades of physical and mental suffering? How could China have achieved these goals?

3. Given the fact that the Chinese government exercised hegemony over the entire Korean peninsula for many centuries and was the wellspring of Korea's traditional culture—not to mention having joined in the North Korean attempt to take over South Korea in the early 1950s—why have the Chinese not played a more aggressive role in helping North Korea overcome its paranoia toward other countries and its obsession with communist ideology?

Looking Out for Number One

Between 1966 and 1976 millions of Chinese died or spent time in slave labor camps and factories. When confronted with the point that so many people were dying, Mao responded that the peasants of China were like weeds—mow them down and they spring right back up.

During that 10-year period, agriculture and industry were mismanaged to the point that the economy was dysfunctional. But this was to change almost magically after China's new chairman Deng Xiaoping announced the beginning of a new era—euphemistically referred to as "socialistic capitalism."

Shortly thereafter, many restrictions that had prevented people from changing jobs and moving away from their birthplaces were lifted. Virtually everyone in the country, from teenagers on up, began to think in terms of what they could do to get a piece of the action.

Literally, for the first time in the history of the country individual Chinese were free to look out for number one, and millions of them began doing so with a vengeance.

The New-Age Entrepreneurs

Within the first year after the beginning of the Deng era there were several hundred thousand new businesses in China—started by individuals who were powered by incredible energy and ambition that had been unleashed for the first time.

What is equally remarkable is that some five percent of these entrepreneurs were women—a figure that was to grow to 20 percent by the end of 1990s and is still growing exponentially.

Today, China is home to some of the richest entrepreneurs in the world—men and women who run international companies that compete head-on with American, European, Japanese, and other foreign enterprises.

Many of the most successful entrepreneurs in China were educated in the United States and are members of the Chinese Entrepreneur Association, which has offices and affiliates in several foreign countries and many international cities.

One of the most outstanding of these billionaire entrepreneurs is Jason Jiang, the founder of Focus Media, a company that places and maintains hundreds of thousands of large video screens in the lobbies and other public areas of buildings throughout China that feature nothing but advertising.

Jiang got the idea for Focus Media in 2002 when staring at an advertising poster on a wall while waiting for an elevator in a Shanghai shopping mall. It occurred to him that a video screen would be far more attractive and appealing than a poster, and within five years had built the idea into a 6-billion dollar-plus advertising network. He was 30 years old when he founded the company.

The use of wall posters as the primary means of public communication had been traditional in China since ancient times, used by the government, by businesses, and by individuals. Prior to Focus Media, there was hardly a wall in China that was not plastered with posters. Now it is flat video screens—and they are one of the most powerful elements in the rapidly changing culture of China.

Among the most prominent advertisers on Jiang's video screens: PepsiCo China, Motorola, Procter & Gamble, KFC, and Armani Cosmetics. As of this writing, he has already spread the concept of public video screen advertising to Hong Kong, Singapore, Taiwan, and Vietnam—bringing the cultural transformation power of his concept to these countries.

DISCUSSION TOPICS & QUESTIONS

Globalization Interest or Self-Interest

1. Do you approve of the fact that Western and other Asian companies have swarmed into China in a virtual stampede—at first to take advantage of cheaper labor and then to make profits from the growing consumer market?

2. What do you think of the fact that by controlling access to their market and both encouraging and subsidizing export industries the Chinese government was able to amass one of the largest hordes of foreign exchange, mostly U.S. dollars, that the world has ever seen—primarily at the expense of the United States?

The New Romans

A growing number of China's entrepreneurial firms have joined the rush to globalize their operations in ways that were not imaginable until the last half of the first decade of the 21st century—a fundamental change spurred by IBM, which led the move to go beyond international branch operations by globalizing their workforce, shunting work in real time to whatever country had the necessary skilled employees—a move that replaced the old foreign branch concept.

Employees of IBM and other international firms that have operating units in China are required to undergo intensive training in Chinese culture—and Chinese employees who are placed in units outside of China undergo similar training in the culture and language of the country they are assigned to.

This extraordinary process is spreading knowledge of Chinese culture abroad as well as introducing more Western cultures into China—an exchange that will go farther than any other effort to create a common international culture and global economy at the same time.

It is especially interesting to note that one of the elements in this globalization of workforces is the presence of a degree of Confucian-style collectivism—an ingredient that Nokia and other such companies have found necessary to bind their diverse collection of workers together.

It is becoming more and more common to find Chinese engineers, technicians, scientists, and other professionals in countries around the world—and like the Romans before them they are taking their culture with them. The number of foreigners studying the Chinese language and Chinese culture has been increasing exponentially since the 1990s.

DISCUSSION TOPICS & QUESTIONS

The Chinese are Here! The Chinese are Here!
1. The foreign exchange amassed by the Chinese government between 1980 and 2000 enabled them to begin a frenzy of buying up rights to raw materials around the world. It also allowed them to dramatically expand their distribution and marketing activities in developed markets worldwide. Do you see this as a good thing?

2. Given the world situation today, suggest new policies and practices that you believe foreign governments should create and implement in their dealings with China.

The New-Age Aristocrats

Successful entrepreneurs in China have become the new aristocrats but they do not owe their success to the government or to aristocratic ancestors. They made their fortunes themselves—another first in the history of China.

These new modern-day mandarins act and live like the newly rich everywhere, with expensive cars, homes, art collections, and many of the other things that are common among the wealthy.

Much of their success was based on the fact that they combined Western technology and management practices with elements of traditional Chinese culture, especially building and using domestic and international networks of connections.

By combining the best of Western and Chinese cultures this new breed of entrepreneurial aristocrats is having a profound impact on the mindset of virtually all Chinese, expanding their horizons beyond the domestic and traditional—a phenomenon that will have a growing impact on the rest of the world.

The New Women of China

One of the most extraordinary changes that have occurred in China is the role of women since 1976—to be more precise, since the communist takeover of China in 1949.

For all of the death, destruction, and suffering Mao Zedong brought to China during his 27-year reign he was a champion of women's rights. He made use of female soldiers and civilians during the long revolution he and his forces fought against the government-aligned Chinese Nationalists. Shortly after taking power in 1949 he gave women the right to vote. Female cadre played an important role in his communist government and both female cadre and female students played key roles in the so-called Cultural Revolution that lasted from 1966 to his death in 1976.

The new Deng era brought more freedom and opportunity to Chinese girls and women. They flocked into universities and factories by the millions, with significant numbers of them starting their own businesses.

As usual in dramatic cultural changes, Chinese girls and women took the lead in adopting American culture, from apparel and cosmetics to fast foods.

By the turn of the 21st century young urban Chinese females were among the most fashionably dressed and made-up women in the world.

Like their Japanese counterparts of the 1960s and 70s this new breed of Chinese girls and women began to imitate the look of foreign fashion models. Large numbers of them began seeking to whiten their skin with various cosmetics and chemicals—some of which proved to be dangerous—and to have the epicanthic fold surgically removed from their eyes to make them "rounder." A few went to serious extremes in an effort to lengthen their legs. The slogan of this new breed was: "Whiter, Skinnier, Taller!"

Chinese women now make up a significant percentage of all employees in government and industry, the latter particularly in such professions as advertising, marketing, public relations, teaching, medicine, and science—not to mention assembly-line manufacturing.

Foreign enterprises with operations in China have found that Chinese women are typically more adaptable and more loyal than male employees, and those who have studied English generally speak it much better than males with the same educational background.

Foreign companies already in China and those proposing to go there would be well advised to make sure that their employee-mix favors the female side.

DISCUSSION TOPICS & QUESTIONS

The Glass-Ceiling in China

1. Until the revolution that ended the last imperial dynasty in China in the early 1900s women played significant roles in the government, serving not only as empresses but as behind-the-scenes consorts, officials, and the wives of officials, exercising great power.

2. Mao Zedong gave ordinary women of China the opportunity to participate in the political life of the country after he took power in 1949. The results were slow in coming but Mao's extraordinary move was to have a profound influence on China following his death in 1976 and the introduction of elements of capitalism and consumerism by his successor.

3. By the 1990s much of the industry of China was running on "female power."

4. By the first decade of the 21st century there were a few high-ranking female officials in China's government. Under what circumstances do you think a woman could emerge as the prime minister of China?

The Influence of American Movies & Television on Chinese Culture

Two other cultural imports from America that were to have a profound influence on the mindset and behavior of young Chinese were American television and American movies. The lifestyles depicted in television shows and in movies—the good, the bad and the ugly—opened the eyes of the young Chinese to a world they had never seen before and in many cases could not even have imagined.

These two imports from America helped put the finishing touches on a new breed of Chinese who were no longer bound by the limitations and restraints of the traditional culture.

As is well known, the influence that American movies have had on the United States has been seriously detrimental to the traditional values and behavior of Americans and this influence is so diverse and so economically powerful that it continues unabated despite widespread public criticism.

It is therefore not surprising that American movies have played a major role in contributing to cultural changes in China. However, from the beginning the communist government of China strictly controlled the kind of movies that could be imported in the country, prohibiting those that were based on violence and overt sexual behavior, attempting to protect young Chinese moviegoers from these influences.

What was fed into the mindset of young Chinese by the movies that were permitted into the country was a lifestyle of personal freedom, attractive clothing, automobiles, entertainment of all kinds, dating, choosing their own spouses, living in their own apartments or homes—and the importance of earning good money in order to afford such things.

With the appearance of American television programs in China the impact on the culture became far more pronounced, as it affected all ages and was programmed into the minds of viewers daily instead of occasionally as in the case of movies in theaters.

The Chinese government has continued to monitor and control the movie and TV fare that is shown in China, but it is now far more lax than in earlier times and will no doubt become less restricted as time passes.

Furthermore, as in the United States and elsewhere, the role of television in the lives of the Chinese soon came under the control of advertisers—a phenomenon that invariably leads to programs appealing to the lowest tastes of viewers. This, combined with the gradual weakening of government controls, makes it virtually inevitably that television programming in China will continue to follow that of the United States, Japan, and other countries.

DISCUSSION TOPICS & QUESTIONS

American Pop Culture vs. China's Traditional Culture

1. Given the debased and destructive elements in much of America's popular culture do you approve of China's efforts to keep this kind of "entertainment" out of the country?

2. Do you think China is making a mistake in gradually relaxing its controls on what entertainment is imported into the country?

China's Sexual Revolution

Prior to the arrival of the American style "get rich" era, the Chinese were known as the Puritans of the East. Premarital sex among young men and women, and cohabitation without marriage, was rare. In the middle and upper classes in particular brides were expected to be virgins.

As in most societies, older urban men of means had access to a variety of women, from female servants to professional "public women," but the overall sexual environment was restrained, obscured, and generally not talked about.

Sex—*xing* (sheeng) in Chinese—is still not commonly talked about in public, but by the turn of the century things had changed dramatically. Social authorities say some seventy percent of urban boys and girls, from high school age on up, now engage in intimate relationships.

There are numerous small hotels, especially in the vicinity of high school and university campuses, that cater almost exclusively to young unmarried couples who rent rooms for one, two, or three hours. The news media has dubbed these trysting places "hookup hotels." The scale of China's "hookup hotel" industry has a long way to go before it catches up with Japan's "love hotels," but it is well on the way.

As in the West, older singles "hook up" for short times or one-night stands at bars and clubs, with older men taking their casual partners to larger and more upscale hotels.

Public prostitutes are visible and active in China's cities despite government efforts to keep all sexual activity behind closed doors.

When the head of New York City's tourism development bureau visited China in 2008 the thing that most of the female journalists who interviewed him were most interested in was the TV show *Sex and the City*. None of them mentioned the Empire State Building or the famous New York department stores.

DISCUSSION TOPICS & QUESTIONS

The Sexing of China

1. Unlike countries in the West and elsewhere that have traditionally attempted to control sexual behavior through religious taboos, China has never had such sanctions. Whether sexual activity in pre-modern China was considered right or wrong depended on who, the place, and the time.

2. Do you believe the Chinese system is more humane, more rational, and therefore superior to religious-based morality? Would you advocate the Chinese way of looking at and engaging in sex being officially adopted in the United States and other Christian and Islamic-oriented countries?

3. Doesn't this system already exists in some Western countries, and isn't it gradually developing in the U.S.? What is your preference?

The Influence of the English Language On Chinese Culture

Even more fundamental than the appearance of a McDonald's in the heart of China were the millions of students who by the mid-1980s were studying the English language as fervently as their ancestors had once studied the *Analects of Confucius*.

Since language is both the reservoir and transmitter of culture, the more English these millions of young Chinese learned the more American culture they absorbed. This not only meant that they became more capable of thinking and acting like Americans, they also became less likely to think and behave in restrictive Confucian terms.

English as it is spoken actually requires rational-logical thinking, and therefore encourages individualism and independence. The difference in the behavior of Chinese (as well as Japanese, Koreans, etc.) who have learned and used a significant amount of English and those who are still monolingual is extraordinary.

Conversing in American English requires these people to step outside of their Chinese skin and immerse themselves in the culture of America. During their early experience with English, they automatically shift back to their native culture when interacting with other Chinese, but with the passing of time the influence of American culture begins to take precedence, and they become less Chinese in their fundamental mindset even when conversing with other Chinese.

The younger the individuals are when they learn and first begin to use English, the faster and more profound the influence of American culture on their thinking and behavior. In children, the change from Chinese-oriented thinking and behavior to American-oriented thinking and behavior is very conspicuous within one to two years.

The cultural changes that occur in the mindset of young Chinese who become fairly fluent in English is so pronounced that it literally de-Chinese-izes them—a phenomenon that is almost instantly detectable by adult Chinese who are still *Chinese* Chinese.

However, unlike the Japanese who are extraordinarily insular when it comes to their culture, and automatically discriminate against Japanese who have become "tainted" by learning English and absorbing American ways, the Chinese are far more open-minded and accepting, and tend to envy rather than harass their English-speaking acquaintances, work associates, and friends.

DISCUSSION TOPICS & QUESTIONS

The Power of the English Language

1. Authorities in various fields tell us that our ability to think complex thoughts depends absolutely on our knowledge of some language—and the more fluent we are in one or more languages, the more ability we have to think.

2. It is apparently not yet well known that learning to speak English fairly fluently influences the values, the attitudes, and the behavior of people. What effect is this having on China?

3. Do you believe that English speaking countries should, as a matter of their foreign policy, officially encourage China to adopt English as its second language? Explain your reasoning.

The Games Kids Play

As already noted the appearance of computers and video games in China—combined with the affluence that made it possible for millions of Chinese families to buy these things for their children—was to become one of the most powerful forces bringing about change in the culture of China.

In another first in the history of the country, millions of young Chinese—especially young Chinese boys—began to spend hours every day glued to video games—games imported from Japan that were based on action, male-female relationships, overt sensuality, cars, weapons and other things that were new to Chinese culture.

The cultural impact that these games have had and are still having on present-day generations of children and preteens is also profound in that the games program them to think and behave in non-Chinese ways.

Video games have not only introduced young Chinese to technology and a world outside of China, increasing their interest in these things, they have also contributed to the number of young people who opt to study English and become involved in international business.

With training in management skills morphing into computerized games (a phenomenon pioneered by L'Oreal and other American multinationals) the skills learned by China's new generation of game players are a major asset when they enter the workforce.

DISCUSSION TOPICS & QUESTIONS

Computer Games Replace Parents

1. There is still debate about the influence that video games have on children, with the industry—not surprisingly—downplaying any negative factors. There is no question that the impact of foreign video games on Chinese children has become a major factor in the culture. Extrapolate on the affect you think this will have in the future on China's cultural as a whole.

2. Do you believe that the Chinese government is justified in trying to control the content of video games imported into the country? Why?

The Influence of Foreign Music

The Chinese learned a long time ago that music has the power to entertain, enthrall and spiritually satisfy people, as well as to incite them to rage and violence of one kind or another when it is misused.

This knowledge led the ancient Chinese to take the rational, positive approach to the creation and use of music as an integral part of their culture. But it also made them far more susceptible to the influence of Western music soon after the new Deng era of personal freedom began.

But by the 1990s large numbers of China's new "get rich quick" generation had succumbed to the powerful influence of popular American music—much of which was anti-almost-everything that was positive about and had distinguished traditional Chinese culture.

There is a positive and a negative side to the popularity of American music among young Chinese. It too, like video games, encourages individualism and independence, which normally adds a very desirable element to human life. But it also adds an element of discontent and blatant criticism that is often without reason and leads to social violence—the antithesis of Confucian philosophy.

DISCUSSION TOPICS & QUESTIONS

The Power of Music

1. Human beings learned very early that the rhythmic beating drums and other kinds of music have a dramatic impact on the nervous system of the body that is reflected both emotionally and intellectually.

2. Do you approve of the appearance of foreign rock bands in China—or anywhere else for that matter?

The Inroads of Western Entertainment in China

By the end of the 20th century bars, cabarets, and nightclubs were as common in mainland China as they had been in Hong Kong since the late 1800s. Today, nightlife in China's major cities rivals that of Bangkok, Seoul, Taipei, and Tokyo, and puts major American and European cities to shame in its volume and variety.

All of the exotic opulence and vices that traditionally characterized nighttime entertainment for the elite in ancient China are once again thriving, and now play a key role in the life of the affluent as well as the elite. Not surprisingly, the entertainment trades were among the first to proliferate and prosper when the era of "get rich" began in the late 1970s.

The impact of the internationalized entertainment industry on Chinese culture is profound, and like the computer and the Internet has changed the once unchangeable culture of China in ways and to a degree that could not have been imagined before the end of the Mao era.

Upscale Chinese nightclubs and other venues are now on the entertainment circuit of American and European performers. Top musical groups from the U.S. and Europe attract audiences in the tens of thousands, some grossing upwards of a million dollars for sell-out concerts.

Many international hotels have their own entertainment centers. Karaoke (*kah-rah-oh-kay...not* kerry-oh-kee!) bars have proliferated. In short, foreign entertainment is one of China's most successful cultural imports, and its impact on Chinese culture is profound.

Nighttime entertainment has traditionally been intimately associated with business relationships in China. Since Western style entertainment is naturally associated with doing business with Westerners, the growth of one is enhancing the growth of the other, adding more fuel to the cultural changes sweeping China, including the internationalization of the economy.

DISCUSSION TOPICS & QUESTIONS

Bars, Nightclubs, and Cabarets

1. Those who have not experienced the nightlife of Bangkok, Hong Kong, or the major cities of Japan, Korea, and China may not appreciate the role it plays in these countries—not only on a personal level but even more importantly on a business and political level.

2. As in the other major cities of Asia, much of the business of China is now conducted after hours in its nighttime trades.

3. What does this tell you about the cultures of China and the other countries that are in the Buddhist and Confucian sphere of Asia?

The Foreign Fast-Food Culture Invades China

Another factor in the rapid diminishing of traditional Chinese culture has been the proliferation of Western-style fast-food restaurants in virtually every nook and cranny of the country.

Chinese style fast-food restaurants—particularly in the form of food-stalls and carts—have been common in China since ancient times, and they still exist in large numbers but during the 1980s and 90s they were joined by a host of American and Japanese fast-food restaurants that have brought about fundamental changes in the physical appearance of Chinese cities as well as the eating habits of huge numbers of Chinese.

In 2005 "life-coach" June Hu wrote an article headlined: *"Forget Politics! U.S. Culture Has Invaded the Mainland and China Will Never Be the Same!"* Hu went on to quote correspondent Stephen Roach that while you usually find a church in the middle of small American and European towns in China you will generally find a Kentucky Fried Chicken or a McDonald's or both.

In addition to these two American icons in virtually every city and town in China you also find Pizza Huts, Wendy's, Swensen's Ice Cream Parlors, Texas Buffet Barbecues and more—not to mention an equal number of huge Japanese fast-food chains such as Mos Burger and Yoshinoya (beef on a bowl of rice).

Like the post-1960 generations of young Japanese before them, the youth of China—and their liberated parents—began flocking to these new restaurants for their foreign ambiance as well as their food. The impact this phenomenon has had on the mindset of the Chinese may be anathema to traditionalists—both Chinese and foreign—but it is the face of the New China.

By the first decade of this century these new imports had begun adding drive-thru windows to accommodate the growing number of Chinese who have cars—not to mention home delivery service for pizzas.

In other words, the exotic image that older foreigners may have of China has been relegated to personal and special events and to the vast Western regions of the country that are not yet in the internationalized mainstream of Chinese life.

And like the young people of Japan, urban Chinese youth do not look upon KFC, McDonald's, and other foreign restaurants as alien. They see them as simply part of the modern Chinese scene.

Another fall-out from the proliferation of American fast-food restaurants has been the appearance of Chinese-owned fast-food chains based on the American concept—exactly the same thing that happened in Japan following the appearance of Big Macs and KFC in that country.

One of the first of these fast-food clones was the cleverly named East Dawning chain, which serves traditional Chinese favorites— fried eel, spicy beef with noodles, crispy wok-fried chicken, ground meat and chicken wings, sweet-and-sour pork ribs, and marinated egg and plum juice.

DISCUSSION TOPICS & QUESTIONS

The Power of Food

1. The power of food to influence the attitudes and behavior of people has long been well known by authorities in several fields, but it has been given little credence or importance by people at large. The American food industry in particularly is notorious for fostering unhealthy foods onto the public—and some of these foods manufacturers are doing the same thing in China.

2. Traditional Chinese food has a history of several thousand years, and over the millennia has been studied and shaped not only by chefs but also by doctors and scientists. Now it has been replaced by foreign foods, especially American, among younger generations of Chinese. Do you approve of this phenomenon? If not, what would you propose be done about it?

The Shopping Scene in Today's China

Just as American, Japanese, and other ethnic food restaurants have changed the eating habits of millions of Chinese as well as the landscape of the country, the shopping scene in larger urban areas in China—from appliances, clothing, computer goods, cosmetics, shoes, soft drinks, to toys—had been internationalized by the first decade of the 21st century.

Every high-end foreign brand that you can name—and many that you may not know—is in China, making shopping there very much like it is in Hong Kong, London, New York, Paris, Rome,

Tokyo, and other leading capitals and regional cities of the world. Foreign residents and visitors to China feel right at home in upscale Chinese boutiques, department stores, pharmacies, and supermarkets.

Want coffee instead of traditional tea or a soft drink? Look for the nearest Starbucks or another Western style coffee shop.

Fashion Boutiques

Visitors who first come across the proliferation of brand-name foreign and Chinese-owned boutique shops in Beijing, Shanghai, and other leading Chinese cities can be forgiven if they get the impression that they are on Nathan Road in Hong Kong, Ginza Street in Tokyo, or Rodeo Drive in Los Angeles.

Upscale shops selling apparel, footwear, accessories, jewelry, and other items with both Chinese and international brands have put yet another face on shopping in China for both residents and visitors alike.

Visitors might want to patronize the shops featuring Chinese-made merchandise rather than more expensive imports, which appeal mostly to well-to-do Chinese shoppers.

Foreign Supermarkets

The mom & pop shops that dominated the Chinese grocery scene for thousands of years now compete with American, French, Japanese, Thai, and other foreign supermarkets that have spread across the vast expanses of China.

These include the American-owned Walmart and Pricesmart chains, the French Carrefour chain, the Japanese Ito-Yokado chain, and the Lotus chain from Thailand.

In addition to imports, these chain stores carry wide selections of domestic foodstuffs, drinks, and other items common in American-style supermarkets.

Earlier predictions by some that foreign style supermarkets would not succeed in China were mistaken. They are just one of the amazing cultural and infrastructural changes that began sweeping the country in the 1980s, and are indicative of the modern consumer market that has developed in China.

The Impact of Foreign Sports on Chinese Culture

Sports of various kinds have been traditional in China since ancient times, with large numbers of amateurs and professionals, the latter staging performances on national, regional, and local levels. Many of these events were on a very large scale, involving hundreds of participants. Professional level training in various sports typically began at a very young age.

Mao Zedong's new People's Republic of China, established in 1949, made the promotion of sports on a national scale an official part of its revolutionary program.

Mao's successors continued this program, and China is now a world-class leader in sports on every level, with extensive programs in every school in the country, amateur teams that participate in the Olympics, and professional teams that play a significant role in the economy and the culture.

American and other Western sports in particular have had a significant impact on Chinese culture—further internationalizing it and pushing traditional culture deeper into the background.

Television was the primary medium by which American sports became popular among the Chinese, first with foreign stars becoming known and admired by Chinese fans and then by the appearance of Chinese stars in the American sports world.

Yao Ming, the extra-tall Shanghai-born basketball player who was drafted by the Houston Rockets in 2002, became an overnight sensation in China, converting millions of Chinese into enthusiastic basketball fans.

In the 1980s and 90s both American and Chinese entrepreneurs went all out to introduce Western sports into the lives of young Chinese. Huge amounts of money were spent advertising sports teams and sporting goods.

These activities not only changed the way millions of Chinese thought about sports in general, it also changed their personal appearance as Western sportswear and jeans became another symbol of the new China.

The Olympic Impact

A sports event that had a far more seminal impact on the whole of China was hosting the Summer Olympics in 2008. Following in the footsteps of Japan in 1964 and South Korea in 1988, China used the Olympics as its coming-out party to graphically demonstrate to the world that the Middle Kingdom was back.

Preparations for the event, which attracted some half a million visitors from abroad, included everything from the construction of spectacular sports venues in Beijing, Shanghai, Qindao, Qinhuangdao, Tianjin, Shenyang, and Hong Kong, to the training of thousands of hotel staff members and Olympic guides in English and in the Western way of greeting and taking care of foreign guests.

Altogether, the government co-sponsored the training of some 400,000 hotel and restaurant employees in English and deportment—a program that contributed significantly to the efforts of large numbers of Chinese to become bilingual for both business and cultural reasons.

The Beijing Foreign Affairs School trained 180 young women to greet foreign VIP guests and to serve as assistants at Olympic awards ceremonies. Impeccably dressed in high-fashion uniforms, these young women helped put a new face on China.

Another series of programs initiated by China's service sector prior to the Olympics was designed to improve public manners. The city of Beijing sponsored a program known as "The Day of Queuing" in an effort to dissuade aggressive people from cutting into lines of those waiting to get into taxis, buses, trains, theaters, sports stadiums, etc.—a traditional custom that foreign visitors found especially upsetting.

Several of the 2008 Olympic venues became instant landmarks, and continue to attract hundreds of thousands of sightseers. The jewel among these spectacular facilities is the National Stadium in Beijing, dubbed "The Bird's Nest" because of its unusual architecture. It seats 80,000 spectators.

DISCUSSION TOPICS & QUESTIONS

The Power of Sports

1. Sports are another cultural activity that has a profound influence on the attitudes and behavior of people. What games people play are, in fact, a kind of Rorschach test of their values and how they treat each other.

2. Traditionally Chinese sports included acrobatics and wrestling. Still today China's young acrobats are internationally famous for their incredible skills.

3. What do the traditional and modern sports of China tell you about Chinese culture?

The Influence of Foreign Celebrities On Chinese Culture

Not surprisingly, one of the most powerful factors in the rapid internationalization of China is the influence that American celebrities have had and continue to have on the mindset of young Chinese.

Ask young Chinese who their favorite celebrities are and they will reel off the names of half a dozen or more American movie and TV stars.

The faces, figures, fashions, and glamorous lifestyles of these celebrities have a seductive appeal to young Chinese, especially girls and young women, who are at the forefront of many of the cultural changes taking place in the country.

This phenomenon is visible in the appearance and behavior of young people—again, especially young women—on shopping streets, in shopping malls, at restaurants, in international hotels and in nightclubs in all of the major cities of China.

This cultural phenomenon is not just casual or cosmetic. It is one of the primary forces impacting China's growing consumer market, spurring its growth and making it international.

American and other foreign companies doing business in China are playing a direct and leading role in this cultural and economic transformation by aiming much of their advertising and other marketing efforts at teenagers and young men and women.

DISCUSSION TOPICS & QUESTIONS

The Celebrity Syndrome

1. "Celebrity worship" has no doubt been around since the beginning of humanity, but it was not until the 20th century and the advent of movies and television that celebrities could be made overnight and their fan base reach millions in a matter of days if not hours. Americans are among the champion celebrity makers, and their worship of celebrities often borders on the rabid. It is also common for Americans to attribute political wisdom to people who are "famous" because they have appeared in a number of popular films and become well known.

2. This phenomenon was exported to Japan in the 1980s and 90s, and is now growing in China. What do you think the overall effect of this will be on China in the future?

The Automobile Culture In China

The appearance of large numbers of automobiles in the United States shortly after the beginning of the 20th century made it possible for both men and women to swiftly and easily travel long distances. Of special significance was the fact that women could travel safely by themselves without being criticized or subjected to any sanctions.

This technological development precipitated a fundamental change in American culture that has not yet run its course—and the same thing is now happening in China. But over time the impact on the culture of China will be even more profound than it was in the United States because the transition from the old to the new has much farther to go.

The entire face of China has changed and is continuing to change with the development of the street, highway, and service infrastructure that is required for an automobile culture. What it has done and is doing to the way the Chinese think and behave constitutes another cultural revolution—one that is also having a direct impact on the rest of the world.

Before the end of the first decade in the 21st century China was already the second largest automobile market in the world. With its one billion-plus population and ongoing economic growth this extraordinary phenomenon was inevitable.

The impact this has had and is having encompasses all areas of Chinese life—culturally, economically, and politically. It addition to programming the Chinese to be more objective and less cultur-ally subjective in all of their affairs, this dramatically new auto-mobile culture is having more and more impact on the rest of the world—from its use of oil and other forms of energy to the supply of other raw materials it needs to sustain the new lifestyle.

DISCUSSION TOPICS & QUESTIONS

Automobiles Drive Cultural Changes

1. In the history of mankind few technological developments have resulted in more fundamental changes in cultures than the appearance of the automobile.

2. These changes are virtually across the board in human behav-ior, impacting on what people do to make a living and how they do it, on the overall infrastructure of their societies, on male-female relationships, and more. The impact that the automo-bile is having on China is not limited to China. It is worldwide and growing.

3. Describe economic, political, and social scenarios that you believe are bound to happen in China in the future as a result of the growing automobile culture. What are some of the changes these developments will have on the rest of the world?

Weddings & Marriage in China

At the beginning of the 21st century, arranged marriages were still a common practice in rural farming areas of China, with elements that had not changed since ancient times, including families "buying" brides for their sons. This practice resulted in an extraordinary number of suicides in these areas, prompting the creation of a number of government agencies and other organizations to combat the problem.

Wedding ceremonies also continue to vary widely in the countryside, with each of the nation's 53 ethnic groups having their own customs, some of which have been traditional for many centuries. Not surprisingly, the more remote and less industrialized these areas the more traditional their marriage customs.

A growing percentage of young urban Chinese in the industrialized areas of eastern and central China make their own decisions about their marriage partners, but many remain family affairs. Wedding ceremonies often include traditional elements— and among the growing number of people who are affluent are typically extravagant. A growing number of the affluent opt for weddings in upscale international hotels.

Virtually all weddings end with a banquet that varies in size and extravagance with the affluence of the two families. Even families in modest financial circumstances typically stage relatively elaborate parties—more because that has been the tradition for a long time than out of any sense of joy or pride.

However, dating and marriage by eligible singles in China is one aspect of the social scene in China that has not been totally transformed by the adoption of Western culture. The percentage of unmarried men and women who are in their late twenties and thirties is apparently the highest in the world—not because the individuals are avoiding marriage but because ongoing social restraints prevent them from finding suitable and willing partners on their own.

The profession of marriage go-between is still flourishing but their services are not always successful and they can be very expensive, especially when they do succeed. In fact, there is a common saying that a go-between who succeeds in getting just one couple married can live for three or four years off of his or her fee.

Online dating services are also active in China, and some appear to be flourishing, but given the ongoing importance of family input in marriages they have not taken off as they did in the United States. This is changing and will change more as the culture is transformed.

Divorce was rare in China until the advent of the communist regime in 1949, at which time revolutionary leader Mao Zedong changed the laws of the land, giving females more of a say in their choice of marriage partners, and making it easier to get a divorce.

Today, divorce in China is becoming more and more common, and there is no longer any serious stigma attached to divorcing and remaining single, or in remarrying.

Resident foreigners and visitors to China frequently encounter wedding parties at the county's leading international hotels. Foreigners who are invited to weddings are invariably briefed on the protocol expected of guests, including the preparation and presentation of gifts of money in red envelopes made for that purpose.

These envelopes, called *hong bao* (hohng bah-oh) in Chinese are available in stationery stores, gift shops, and other outlets. They are also used on other occasions when money gifts are common—funerals, birthday celebrations, and as bonuses to employees at the end of the year (in the latter case, checks may be given instead of cash).

At weddings and other formal events there is normally a table set up, with one or more attendants, near the entrance of the facility where guests presents the *hong bao*.

DISCUSSION TOPICS & QUESTIONS

Traditional and Democratic Marriage Customs

1. The Westernization of dating and marriage customs in China are powerful indicators of the extent to which Western ways have changed Chinese behavior. However, given the Chinese

penchant for elaborate spectacles when it comes to weddings, even among the poor, Western style wedding ceremonies tend to be more elaborate than such events in the West.

2. What does this say about the mindset of the Chinese?

Traditional Medicine in China Today

For well over two thousand years medical practices in China were the most advanced in the known world, with both a physical and metaphysical component. Although modern Western medicine is now widely practiced in China, the use of traditional treatments continues to thrive.

The basic theory of traditional Chinese medicine attempts to explain the nature of the life cycle and bodily changes that result in diseases. It includes five theories: Yin and yang (the positive-negative balance in nature), the five elements (earth, fire, metal, wood, and water), how to direct one's inner strength, the internal body organs, and the "channels" that carry energy throughout the body. In addition to attempting to explain why diseases occur, it included how to diagnose and prevent diseases, and how to keep the body healthy.

Chinese doctors used the yin and yang concept to illustrate the complicated relationship between the different parts of the human body. They became aware a long time ago that maintaining a relative balance in the functions of the body was essential in warding off diseases and staying in good health

By equating the functions of the body with the nature and role of water, fire, metal, and earth they were able to apply the dynamic processes, functions, and characteristics in the natural world to the human body. Their understanding of the inter-relationship between these five elements, how they supported and controlled each other, allowed them to see the parallels in human health.

Just as things go wrong when there is an imbalance in nature, diseases occur when just one element in the body gets out of balance—an imbalance that could be seen in the color of the face, the sound of the voice, and in the emotional state of the individual, and so on.

Chinese doctors determined that when any one of the five solid "yang" organs of the body—spleen, heart, lungs, liver, and kidneys—malfunctioned, that is, got out of its natural yin-yang balance, the individual would suffer from both physical and mental problems.

Likewise, when one or more of the six hollow "yin" organs of the body—small intestines, large intestines, gall bladder, stomach, and a three-part invisible metabolizing agent—malfunctioned it also resulted in some kind of ailment.

An understanding of the channels, or meridians, by which the *qi* (chee) or energy of life, powered these various organs, plus the blood vessels that carried nutrients and oxygen to them and maintained the conductivity of the channels, allowed the Chinese to create exercises and recipes for foods and potions that helped keep all of the body's elements in balance.

The Western world is just now beginning to accept this view of the body and disease, but so far it has not penetrated into the mainstream of Western medicine.

In the 1990s Chinese doctors and scientists, with government backing, began a program of research to understand *qi* in scientific terms—first to prove that it exists and then to devise more remedies based in keeping the energy in balance and returning it to its optimal state when it becomes unbalanced.

In recent decades there have been a number of highly publicized incidents in which Westerners who became ill in China were successfully treated by Chinese doctors using traditional methods. Over time much of the ancient medical wisdom of China may very well come to be accepted by the West.

The Marvel of Acupuncture

The Chinese practice of acupuncture (*zhōn jiu*/june jew) has, in fact, already gained an impressive foothold in the West, particularly in the United States, where there are practitioners in virtually every city.

The number of English-language articles and books on acupuncture is growing exponentially. Mostly written by people with medical backgrounds, the material ranges from descriptions of the basic procedure to its metaphysical implications.

Noted writer and academic Robert Todd Carroll describes the basics of acupuncture as: "Acupuncture is a traditional Chinese medical technique for unblocking *ch'i* or *qi* (chee) by inserting needles at particular points on the body to balance the opposing forces of yin and yang. Chi is an energy that allegedly permeates all things. It is believed to flow through the body along 14 main pathways called meridians. When yin and yang are in harmony, chi flows freely within the body and a person is healthy. When a person is sick, diseased, or injured, there is an obstruction of chi along one of the meridians. Traditional Chinese medicine has identified some 500 specific points where needles are to be inserted for specific effects."

Carroll goes on to note that acupuncture has been practiced in China for more than 2,000 years, and that today, the needles are twirled, heated, or stimulated with weak electrical current, ultrasound, or certain wavelengths of light. He adds that some practitioners use tuning forks over the "acupoints," while others direct laser beams at them or apply magnetic BBs on patches to them.

He summarizes his comments by saying that scientific research has not been able to demonstrate that acupuncture, or "unblocking *qi* by any means," is effective against any disease.

Traditionalists in the Western medical fraternity generally continue to discount the efficacy of acupuncture, but a practice that has survived for millennia is not likely to disappear because of such sentiments among doctors who are slow to doubt their own traditions of medicine.

There are dozens of schools and dozens of thousands of practitioners of acupuncture throughout China, providing interested visitors with an opportunity to view as well as try an acupuncture treatment.

Those who opt to try an acupuncture treatment should keep in mind that it is not a fast-acting miracle cure for any ailment or disease. Most treatments require several sessions, and in more serious cases may go on for months.

Of course, the one area of acupuncture treatment that most foreigners are familiar with is using it (instead of drugs) to block pain during operations. There is copious evidence that it actually works, although most Western doctors and health professionals generally say there is no basis for such a belief and that what is experienced and witnessed is a placebo effect.

DISCUSSION TOPICS & QUESTIONS

What the West Can Learn from China

1. If you have not had an acupuncture treatment would you consider having one?

2. Do you believe there is such a thing as *qi* (chee)—a kind of energy that flows through and animates the body?

The Ongoing Importance of Traditional Music

Ancient people all over the world learned very early that music, in whatever form, has a powerful and fundamental affect on the nervous system, the emotions, and the intellect of human beings, and long before the development of civilization music was an important part of their existence.

While the educated and those in power in early Western civilizations maintained and added to the folk music they inherited from their ancient ancestors there was no overall concerted effort to integrate music into the culture of common people, and even now a significant percentage of Westerners grow up without having the full benefits of music in their lives.

The Chinese, on the other hand, with their long, continuous history were wise enough to take full advantage of the benefits of music. By the emergence of the first dynasties some five thousand years ago, music was a primary and formal part of the lives of the Chinese.

All of the great sages who came afterward, including Confucius in the 5th century B.C. and Mencius who followed him, extolled the importance of music, and taught that it should be an integral part of government as well as the lives of ordinary people. The short-lived *Qin* Dynasty (221-207 B.C.) created an Imperial Music Bureau that was to become a permanent part of the following dynasties.

At first, traditional Chinese music may not appeal to the ears of Westerners but with time it grows on one. Chinese opera and other musical events offer visitors an opportunity to experience one of the most extraordinary elements of Chinese culture. As noted earlier, I especially recommend that visitors attend at least one of China's classic opera performances as well as a performance with a modern theme.

Those who are not familiar with the therapeutic effects of good music as well as its positive mood-enhancing attributes might want to take a page from Chinese culture by making such music a part of their lives.

DISCUSSION TOPICS & QUESTIONS

The Influence of Good Music

1. One of the areas of China's traditional culture that continues to flourish is the presence of and the appreciation of its traditional forms of music. Most Chinese, including younger generations, still have some knowledge of the country's traditional forms of music and continue to appreciate their value.

2. Contrast the ongoing presence and appreciation of traditional music in China with what exists in your own country.

The Cultural Role of China's Traditional Games

Millions of people around the world are familiar with one of China's oldest and most sophisticated board games, but they know it by its Japanese name *Go*, rather than its Chinese name, *Weiqi* (way-chee).

Weiqi developed in China some 3,500 years ago, was introduced into Korea more than 2,000 years ago and brought to Japan around the 13th century A.D.—reportedly by Buddhist priests who went to China to study.

Centuries later, during the heyday of Japan's samurai shogunate era, the game became what amounted to the official pastime of the educated and elite in the samurai class. During the Tokugawa Shogunate (1603-1867), the shoguns themselves were its most prominent boosters.

Weiqi is intellectually demanding, like the Western game of chess, and has long been used as a training tool for military strategists and others (although Confucius is said to have regarded it as a waste of time!).

The leader of China's communist revolution, Mao Zedong, required his generals to study and practice *weiqi*, but when he inaugurated the so-called Cultural Revolution in 1966 in an effort to destroy the Confucian-oriented culture he condemned *weiqi* as a pastime of intellectuals whom he regarded as enemies of the communist ideology.

After the end of the disastrous Cultural Revolution in 1976 (when Mao died) and the gradual recovery of the Chinese economy many older Chinese got their *weiqi* boards out and took up the game again. It has long since been fully rehabilitated and is one of the favorite recreational and training activities of the Chinese.

Playing the game well requires the use of holistic-type thinking that does not come easy to most straight-line thinking Westerners—and is therefore an excellent training tool for those who want to enhance their thinking ability.

The Ubiquitous Mahjong

Mahjong is probably the best known of the games that originated in China—and is still played by large numbers of people as a recreational activity as well as a gambling game.

There are several stories about the origin of mahjong, including one that attributes it to the great sage Confucius in the 5th century B.C. But it is fairly reliably dated as having originated in the 19th century, when historical records note its use for the first time. It is believed that it was developed from an old Chinese card game.

Interestingly, mahjong playing was banned by the communist regime in 1949 because of its connection with gambling. But it has since been revived and is as popular as ever, both as recreation and for gambling. (The game was first played in the U.S. in the 1920s, and now has many devotees. It is also played in many other countries.)

Mahjong is easy to learn, and the ceramic tiles that make up the pieces used, with their colorful ideographic characters, add both a visual and tactile attraction to its appeal.

Like China's famous *Tai Ji Quan* physical exercise that one sees in vacant lots, parks, and other public places in China, large numbers of Chinese, especially elderly men, can be seen playing mahjong in public, often on boards and tables set up on street sidewalks.

DISCUSSION TOPICS & QUESTIONS

Intellectual Games and the Chinese

1. With a history of cultural and technological achievements for well over three thousand years China has produced some of the world's greatest scholars and philosophers. This led to the development of *weiqi*, or *go*, as it is known outside of China, which is said to be more complex than the Western game of chess.

2. What factors in Chinese culture do you think are responsible for the popularity of intellectual games?

3. What reasons suggest that experience in playing chess would be a significant advantage for Westerners negotiating with Chinese, or for military strategists planning for war?

Rehabilitation of China's Ancient Philosophers

Well before the end of the 20th century China's communist rulers began a discreet but public campaign to reverse a policy instituted by the late Chairman Mao Zedong in 1966 to eliminate Confucianism from Chinese culture. This new breed of leaders began the process of partially rehabilitating Confucius—a wise move designed to take advantage of a number of Confucian principles that were compatible with their goals.

Mao had became so frustrated with his failure to wean the Chinese away from the Confucian-oriented culture of the past and convert them to communism that in 1966 he unleashed a "cultural revolution" aimed at destroying all of the traditional beliefs and practices.

Mao turned to the disaffected youth of China to achieve his goal, creating a huge army of "Red Guards" who were brainwashed in his concept of communist ideology and turned loose on the educated and on the property and business owning classes with a mandate to convert them to communism or destroy them.

Millions of high school and university-age students began a wild rampage of burning shrines, temples, libraries, and books, subjecting millions of people to intimidation, torture, and slave labor, and forcing millions into the countryside where huge numbers of them died.

No educated person was safe. Even wearing eyeglasses was enough to get one labeled an intellectual and therefore an enemy of the communist regime.

Mao's spleen was especially directed toward the teachings of Confucianism and other noted philosophers of the past because the principles and practices they taught were often contrary to his communist ideology.

Despite the level of death and destruction that Mao's Red Guards inflicted on China the philosophies of the ancient masters were not entirely consigned to the dust-heap of history, even among some of Mao's own stalwarts.

Mao's attempts to discredit the teachings of Confucius were ostensibly successful among China's student population, but not among the older generations. If they had survived the purges, exile, imprisonment, and executions that befell the educated and property-owning class they kept their beliefs to themselves to avoid such serious consequences.

After the practical-minded Deng Xiaoping, Mao's successor, sanctioned the introduction of government-controlled capitalism and a market economy in the late 1970s, he also let it be known that there were many aspects of Confucianism that were positive and beneficial to Chinese society. By the mid-1980s the gradual rehabilitation of Confucius was well underway.

Hu Jintao, who became General Secretary of the Communist Party in 2002 and the President of China in 2003, based much of his political philosophy on the teachings of Confucius, particularly the importance of maintaining social harmony. From 2005 on, both he and then Premier Wen Jiabao began quoting Confucius to party officials.

Hu frequently referred to the Confucian concept of *hexie shehui* (huh-shay shuu-whay), or "a harmonious society," as "something to be cherished." They also frequently used another Confucian slogan, *heping jueqi* (huh-peng jway-chee), or "peaceful rise," referring to China's policy of growing its economy and position in the world by peaceful means.

In the words of Orville Schell, the Arthur Ross Director of the Center on U.S.-China Relations at the Asia Society, China's leaders now depend on both the ancient wisdom of Confucius and communist doctrine in shaping their policies and goals.

Not surprisingly, the communist leaders appreciate the Confucian concept of respect for and obedience to government authorities. (The fact that this concept included the proposition that rulers should be humane and above reproach was another matter.)

The continuing growth of China's economy in all areas makes the merits of the communist-Confucian approach obvious. As long as this two-cultured policy continues to fulfill the needs and wants of a growing percentage of China's huge population the chances of it surviving into the future are very good.

On the surface, modern urban Chinese culture no longer looks either communist or Confucian. It is, in fact, looking more and more like a clone of the American lifestyle, with all of our free-wheeling ways, excesses, and glitter because young people—both males and females—look upon the American way as preferable to the old ways.

This has not meant—and will not mean—the total disappearance of traditional Chinese culture, but it already means that traditional Chinese attitudes and behavior in the industrialized areas of the country are generally followed and seen only in private situations—in the homes of older people; among traditional artists and craftsmen; in the fields of traditional entertainment, particularly in the theater; during festivals, and such life passage events as traditional weddings, auspicious age celebrations, and funerals.

DISCUSSION TOPICS & QUESTIONS

Return of the Master

1. Despite the efforts of Mao Zedong to eliminate the influence of Confucianism in the Chinese mindset enough of it survived to still be discernible in the character of the Chinese, including those who have been "Westernized."

2. What aspects of Confucianism do you believe will survive in Chinese culture for the foreseeable future, despite the inroads being made by Western concepts and customs?

3. Would you agree that there are aspects of Confucianism that should be integrated into Western cultures?

Education in China

When the People's Republic of China was founded by Mao Zedong in 1949 eighty percent of the Chinese population was mostly or completely illiterate. Less than five percent of the young people in the country were enrolled in schools.

In fact, throughout China's long history the majority of the rural population received little if any formal education, not by choice but because of the culture that favored the middle and upper class—something that Mao was determined to change.

By the end of 1997 the illiteracy rate had dropped to 12 percent and it is now below six percent—a rate that is similar to other advanced countries around the world. Enrollment in elementary schools is said to be 98.9 percent.

On-the-job, long-distance training and continuing education programs are common in China, and nationwide teacher training programs are also in place.

China has student exchange and cooperative relationships with more than 150 countries and regions. Hundreds of thousands of Chinese now study abroad annually, and dozens of thousands of foreign students study in China.

Overall, Chinese students are far more diligent in their studies than Western students—a factor that is playing and may continue to play a significant role in the emergence of China as a superpower.

DISCUSSION TOPICS & QUESTIONS

The Power of Knowledge

1. Perhaps more than most other people, the Chinese of all social levels have long recognized the power of education. The fact that the country was traditionally ruled by a small group of educated bureaucrats, and that the opportunity for education was generally denied to farmers and the menial working class, resulted in the desire for an education among the masses becoming an obsession because it meant power.

2. How does the Chinese obsession with learning equate with the propensity in the West—especially in the United States—for the lower working classes to downplay the importance of education and to look upon going to school as an interference in their lives and to show a lack of respect for those who study hard and are smarter than the average?

3. Why do you think working-class Americans, and many others throughout the world, have historically showed little or no interest in education?

The Tourism Welcome Mat Helping to Save China's Traditional Culture

One of the factors that has played a significant role in the modernization of Chinese culture and the Chinese economy is the national program to attract foreign tourists—a policy that is also playing a key role in preserving many facets of China's traditional culture.

The Chinese have always welcomed foreign guests who came to admire the amazing scenery, technological accomplishments, and traditional cultural attractions of the country—and these things still today draw millions of visitors to China every year.

But to accommodate the millions of visitors China has had to Westernize its infrastructure to an amazing degree—with thousands of high-rise hotels and hundreds of thousands of foreign-styled restaurants and shops, not to mention buses, subways, trains, and more and more highways.

One of the results of all this modernization is that it tends to obscure many of the traditional elements of Chinese culture that are what attracts tourists to China in the first place.

Both the national government and local governments are aware of this dichotomy and go out of their way to protect and promote the most important of the cultural artifacts, events, arts, and crafts that tourists come to see and experience. This mutually beneficial program links the ministry of tourism with hundreds of villages and towns throughout China with the same goals in helping to ensure their survival.

The historical image of China as one of the world's most exotic countries will no doubt continue to persist in the minds of most Westerners for several more generations, and this alone should be enough to continue luring large numbers of visitors to China.

This means, however, that visitors who want to see and experience traditional China must be prepared to travel outside of Beijing, Shanghai, and other modern cities to the countryside, and especially to the provinces and regions of Western China. These cities have their famous contemporary and ancient landmarks, but they are reflections of old China—not the China of today.

Other factors that visitors should be prepared for are the large crowds that swarm shopping areas, transportation terminals, and the modes of transformation, along with the possibility that people in these crowds can be rude by foreign standards. (Still today traditional Chinese etiquette generally applies only to family members, friends, work-related acquaintances, and government officials—not to strangers with whom they have no relationship.)

In the 1990s the national government as well as regional and local governments began sponsoring ongoing poster and television campaigns in an effort to improve the level of public behavior in China.

DISCUSSION TOPICS & QUESTIONS

Tourism as a Cultural Force

1. Tourism is one of the world's largest and most influential industries, and yet in most countries it still does not have the official standing of such things as manufacturing and marketing products. Why is this so?

2. Japanese leaders on the highest level were apparently the first to understand the importance of tourism, and Japan was the first country in the world to have a highly integrated and efficiently run tourism industry on a national level, going back to the early 1600s. Most of the impetus for this remarkable development came from the precepts of Shinto and Buddhism.

3. China's second generation of post-Mao leaders was quick to see the economic importance of tourism, and made it a national effort. Do you believe they understood—and anticipated—the impact that mass tourism would have on the culture of China?

4. Enumerate some of the more basic changes that hordes of foreign tourists descending on China have already had on the infrastructure and economy as a whole, and how it is affecting the mindset of the people.

The Weather in China

The weather in China is very much like that of the United States—a continental monsoon climate with enormous variety. The climate in northern China goes from temperate to frigid, and is typically windy and dry. The climate in the south goes from subtropical to tropical and is generally warm and humid. There are clear divisions between the seasons in the central and northern regions of the country. The climate also varies widely with the topography and distance from the ocean and high mountain ranges. Sand storms are common in western regions, and the higher you get on the Qinghai-Tibet plateau the colder it is at night and in winter. The rainy season runs from May through August, and typhoons are frequent along the southeast coast between July and September.

Smoking in China

In 1995 the Chinese government banned smoking in hospitals, nurseries, primary and secondary schools, theaters, libraries, stadiums, museums, banks, post offices, shops, and all means of public transport. Taxis were later added to this ban. The movement is growing to add additional areas to these bans. Some restaurants in China have instituted their own smoking bans, with mixed results.

China's Gambling Culture

Gambling has been an integral part of Chinese culture since ancient times. In fact, lotteries were used in China some 3,000 years ago to help fund the building of the Great Wall. During some of the long dynasties gambling became so rampant that the government took such extreme measures as chopping the hands off of gamblers and periodically executing large numbers of them.

None of these measures proved to be effective very long. In 1886 the last Imperial Dynasty tried again to curtail the number of lotteries, saying they were similar to robbery and prostitution, and banning them.

The edict slowed lotteries down across the country but they continued to flourish in the treaty ports and in the International Settlement in Shanghai. In 1949 the new communist regime of Mao Zedong outlawed all gambling, but it continued underground.

Other attempts to control gambling in China occurred in 2005, with harsher penalties and inspection teams sent out to the provinces. These efforts have mostly concentrated on government officials accused of gambling with public funds, but overall the government has been ambivalent about the practice and it is either legalized or permitted in the special zones of Hong Kong and Macau as well as areas of the mainland.

So-called "friendly games" of gambling in the country's thousands of mahjong parlors and "social lotteries" have informal approval from top government officials.

Organized gambling in casinos, lotteries, and horseracing is big business, with the local governments getting a substantial piece of the action. All indications are that illegal gambling in China has continued to grow, especially in casinos in areas not under direct control by the national government and despite attempts to use visa-controls to monitor the hundreds of thousands of people who flock to border-town gambling emporiums.

Present-day illegal gambling in China mainly involves Internet betting, so-called private lotteries, and underground casinos, with periodic crackdowns making hardly a dent in the amount of money that changes hands. Visitors to China are cautioned to be wary of gambling in underground places that could be raided.

Big-time Chinese gamblers are frequent visitors to the Casinos of Macau and Las Vegas.

DISCUSSION TOPICS & QUESTIONS

Why Gambling?

1. The urge to gamble has been a common trait in the character of the Chinese since ancient times. What are some of the probable reasons why this is so?

2. Do you think that the gradual introduction of personal freedom in China and the growing number and variety of economic opportunities will dampen the age-old impulse of the Chinese to gamble? Explain.

The New Look of China's Military Forces

Another conspicuous and impressive factor in the present-day cultural facade of China is the new look of the military forces—which as noted earlier owns and operates the largest number of commercial enterprises of any group in the country.

In sharp contrast to the drab uniforms that were long associated with China's military forces, the airmen, soldiers and sailors of present-day China are now among the sharpest dressed military forces in the world, thanks to the military and government decision to hire some of the leading fashion designers and spend several million dollars on new uniforms over the year leading up to the 2008 Summer Olympics that took place in Beijing, Shanghai, and other venues in the country.

Another military policy implemented shortly after the turn of the century was recruitment efforts aimed at college graduates that included higher salaries, other financial and housing perks, and financing for graduate studies after their military service—all aimed at attracting well-educated and technology savvy people needed for the transformation of the military from its historical emphasis on huge numbers of infantry troops to smaller high-tech-based forces.

This too, was seen as making a major contribution to changing the image of the military forces from that of simply enforcing government political policies to socially responsible organizations that served the people during natural disasters and took part in nation-wide greening projects.

DISCUSSION TOPICS & QUESTIONS

A New Face for China's Military

1. The makeover of the uniforms of China's armed forces was of great importance politically as well as culturally. It was a significant sign that the leaders had evolved to the point where they could give human feelings, needs and aspirations precedence over political ideology.

2. What are some of the ramifications of this very conspicuous change in the face of China?

PART IV

Key Words that Reveal the Chinese Way Of Thinking & Behaving

All languages are reflections of the emotional, intellectual, and spiritual character of the people who created them, and the older, more structured and more exclusive a society and its language, the more terms it has that are pregnant with cultural nuances that control the attitudes and behavior of the people.

Here are introductions to a selection of culturally-oriented Chinese terms that are especially important in understanding and dealing with the way the Chinese think and behave.

Bao (Bah-oh)/Trading Social Credits

In societies that do not have laws that allow people to deal with each other in an honest and fair way, relationships of all kinds—business, personal, political, etc.—must be based on trade-offs of one kind or another.

This means that people must first develop personal contacts and then all of the skills that are necessary to accomplish the results they want.

In China this cultural factor is known as *bao* (bah-oh), which may be translated as "social reciprocity."

Despite the fact that the younger generations of Chinese, especially those with international educations, are gradually breaking away from the restraints of *bao* in order to deal more effectively with foreigners, the use of "social credits" continues to play an important role in all aspects of life and work in China.

It is still advisable for foreigners assigned to China to build up *bao* with business contacts and government officials as rapidly and as widely as possible. Just as in the U.S. and elsewhere, one of the primary ways of building up *bao* in China is hosting dinner and drinking parties.

Bi (Bee)/Unity the Chinese Way

The fact that many of the greatest feats of mankind (building long canals, constructing great walls, creating thousands of full-sized terra cotta images of warriors to bury with a dead emperor, etc.) were accomplished in China suggests that the Chinese long ago mastered the art of working together harmoniously and cooperatively.

But this image of China can be misleading to Westerners who are not familiar with the details of Chinese history or with the way the Chinese work together.

In reality the Chinese have always been independent-minded and individualistic but historically they were under the iron fist of rulers who treated them like cattle, forcing them to behave and work in unison to survive.

Chinese philosophers preached about the wisdom of *bi* (bee) or "unity" and the rulers took their preaching to heart, but they used force to compel people to behave the way they wanted them to. And thus the *bi* of China was mostly a mirage.

Now that the heavy boot of the government is gradually being removed from the necks of the Chinese they are exercising various degrees of freewill for the first time in their history, with the result that life in China has become more chaotic than ever before except in times of war.

Most Chinese are now out to get as rich as possible as quickly as possible, resulting in a lot of friction and frustration that alarms the government—and makes the lives of foreigners living and working in China a lot more unpredictable and interesting.

It is therefore important for foreigners in China to be aware of the historical role of Chinese style *bi*, and to use the term in its modern sense in their relationships with Chinese.

Budan Xin (Buu-dahn Sheen)/Chinese Style Sincerity

In China, as everywhere else in the world, people are very much concerned about sincerity in all of their relationships—because without it one's trust can be misplaced and abused with serious consequences.

But problems often occur in cross-cultural relationships despite the fact that both sides are aware of the importance of sincerity and often harp on it in their presentations to each other.

Friction and frustration often occur between the parties for the simple reason that their cultural understanding of sincerity differs in a fundamental way.

The Chinese commonly use the term *budan xin* (buu-dahn sheen) in their references to sincerity and in their desire to have *budan xin* relationships with their foreign business contacts. This, of course, is always pleasing to the foreigners, and they readily agree that they too want sincerity with their business dealings.

These relationships are seldom without misunderstanding and friction, however, because in its Chinese context *budan xin* means "sincerity plus understanding"—and the catch is that this understanding means that foreigners are expected to understand the circumstance or position of the Chinese side, and accept it.

This, of course, puts an entirely different slant on the concept of sincerity that prevails in the West, and it often happens that foreigners dealing with the Chinese must compromise their expectations and behavior to some degree...if they want to do business with them.

Buhe Luoji De (Buu-hay Loo-oh-jee Duh)/Look Out for Fuzzy Logic!

There are three kinds of logic in China: traditional, Communist, and Western—and you have to know which one you are dealing with to understand what is going on.

Until the latter part of the 20th century Chinese in general were not allowed to behave in purely Western style logical ways, despite the fact that they could and did think logically in the Western sense in virtually all matters.

This situation is further complicated in present-day China by the fact that people who have been educated and trained to think and behave logically in Western terms will often behave in the traditional Chinese way by choice or in the Communist way because they have no choice.

The traditional Chinese way of thinking is what I call "fuzzy logic," meaning that it is not the hard two times two equals four kind of thinking or straight-line thinking. It is "holistic" thinking, or thinking in circles.

Since few Westerners are experienced in holistic or circular thinking, Chinese attitudes and behavior are often confusing to them. But fuzzy thinking (the term was actually invented by an American) is often far more powerful than "straight-line" thinking because it takes in a lot more territory in terms of time, space, and long-term results.

Westerners dealing with the Chinese should prepare themselves by learning how to use fuzzy logic.

Buzhidao (Boo-jee-dah-oh)/Avoiding Responsibility!

From the adoption of Confucianism as the law of the land the Chinese were programmed to believe in and accept the idea that collective responsibility took precedence over personal responsibility—which, in fact, was made virtually taboo.

When Chairman Mao Zedong and his cohorts took over China in 1949 and imposed a strict communist regime on the country they not only continued the collective responsibility concept they made it even more comprehensive and imposed even stronger sanctions on people who did not follow its dictates.

These two cultural influences resulted in the Chinese being extremely sensitive about accepting or presuming to accept personal responsibility for virtually any situation or event that had the slightest chance of resulting in some kind of backlash.

This resulted in the phrase *buzhidao*, literally "I don't know," with the added nuances of "I don't care" and "Don't bother me!" becoming one of the most commonly used expressions in the country.

The simplest and most innocuous questions were typically, and often automatically, answered with *buzhidao*, even when there was no danger of any kind. This was especially true during the Mao era when the whole country was made paranoid by the extreme measures the government took to enforce the communist ideology, including encouraging and often requiring people to spy on each other and report even the slightest hint of subversion to the authorities.

The use of *buzhidao* has diminished significantly in recent decades among ordinary people, but it is still a factor in Chinese life, particularly when someone is asked about something or to do something that they do not consider one of their specific duties or functions.

Government officials have long been notorious for using the expression to avoid taking on new responsibility, especially from mid-afternoon on when they don't want anything to interfere with their leaving the office for the day.

This is one of the reasons why things tend to move more slowly in China than elsewhere. Generally speaking, there is no easy or fast solution to this cultural behavior unless you are in a position to insist or otherwise intimidate individuals who don't know, don't want to try to find out, or really don't want to be bothered.

Fortunately, younger Chinese, especially those who have studied English and are more internationally oriented, will typically go out of their way to help foreigners.

This said, it is still important to keep in mind that except in rare and relatively recent cases individual Chinese generally do not take personal responsibility for their actions. Theirs is generally a world of mutual responsibility, and works primarily on a consensus basis—forced or unforced.

The difference between the mutual responsibility of Chinese and the individual responsibility of Americans and others has profound implications when it comes to doing business with each other.

There is no simple solution to these cultural differences. Generally speaking, the Chinese (as well Japanese, Koreans, and other Asians) must act as a team or the whole structure falls apart.

It is wise for individualistic Westerners to take the team approach in China and in other Asian countries where business is more subjective and more group-oriented.

Cheng (Chuung)/The Importance of Personal Loyalty

Westerners are, of course, familiar with the concept of personal loyalty and are well aware of how important it can be in their lives. But their concept of the importance of personal loyalty pales when compared with that of the Chinese.

Again because the Chinese have never been able to depend upon their governments to detail and defend their rights with laws that applied to everyone, they have been on their own when it comes to avoiding problems, protecting themselves and surviving in every sense of the word.

This situation has changed considerably in present-day China, but the average Chinese still has to depend upon the personal loyalty of family and friends to a far greater extent than Americans and other Westerners.

The Chinese therefore put great credence in developing and sustaining relationships that are based on strong *cheng* (chuung) ties. This requirement takes up a great deal of the time and energy of the Chinese when both of the parties involved are Chinese.

Interestingly enough, the Chinese can often develop strong *cheng* relationships with foreigners faster than they can with other Chinese because the cultural baggage that comes with Chinese relationships is far heavier.

Some Chinese/foreign relationships between businesspeople have survived time and war and become legendary.

Chou (Choh-ou)/Criticism is Not Taken Lightly!

Americans typically have thick skins when it comes to criticism. Most can take a lot of it before being aroused to any kind of action. In addition to being culturally programmed to take the position that we are right and the critics are wrong; or to respond with a "so what" attitude, we are also programmed to give as good as we get when the going really gets rough.

Chinese culture is the reverse of this thick-skinned in-your-face approach to criticism. Their prime rule for millennia was harmony—virtually at whatever cost. Social and political stability came before the personal feelings of individuals.

The traditional Confucian-based harmony that was the official policy of the imperial government was embedded in the etiquette, and controlled all behavior—emotional, intellectual, spiritual, and physical.

Life was scripted down to the last detail. Failure to observe all of the rules of etiquette was a serious breach of morality, and could have very serious consequences.

This virtual obsession with proper behavior made the Chinese extraordinarily sensitive to what was colloquially referred to as *chou*, which actually means "stinky" or "smelly." Superiors could criticize inferiors, but not the other way around.

It became taboo to criticize parents, educators, public officials, and government leaders—a system that was designed to maintain absolute harmony, but did so on the surface only. Below the surface people seethed with emotional, physical, and intellectual frustration.

When the Communists first took over China Chairman Mao continued this policy of prohibiting criticism of the Party and its members, but some years later he rescinded the taboo and announced a policy of "letting a million flowers bloom" (or words to that effect), but the outpouring of criticism was such that he quickly reinstated the ban.

There has since been a significant change in the role of *chou* in China, but only in some areas. Criticism of the government is still considered treasonous and results in arrest and long prison terms. However, criticism by government leaders and officials of both private individuals and companies as well as government officials who misbehave or fail in their duties is rampant.

Individuals as well as the news media are now free to criticize, and they do so with gusto. But criticism on an individual level can be dangerous. Criticizing someone directly is still considered uncivilized and insulting, and almost always results in the offended party seeking to take some kind of revenge against the perpetrator.

Foreign residents and visitors should be wary of publicly criticizing any aspect of the Chinese government as well as openly criticizing employees or business contacts. Criticizing someone, when it is deserved, should be done privately and diplomatically.

Daoqian (Dow-chee-inn)/The Importance of the Apology

Apologies are an important element in all societies but they are even more important in China and other Asian countries in the Confucian sphere of influence, particularly Japan and Korea, where people are exceptionally sensitive to anything that causes them embarrassment or any kind of problem.

Because of this the Chinese and other Asians apologize in serious situations and in minor situations that Westerners are likely to ignore. They also apologize when they are not guilty of anything!

Traditionally an apology was often the only recourse that the Chinese and other Asians had because there were no laws or cultural rules to protect them.

Apologies in China therefore carry greater weight than they do in Western societies. In many cases a humble apology is often enough to get one out of a relatively serious situation.

On the other hand, refusing to apologize when an apology is expected and/or is actually called for can be very serious indeed because it is taken as an aggressive act.

Foreigners who break a law in China are invariably better off if they apologize quickly. There are also numerous occasions, including very minor ones, when an apology is in keeping with the cultural expectations of the Chinese and is a good thing to do.

De (Duh)/The Saving Grace of Humanity

In the 5th century B.C. the Chinese philosopher Lao Tzu began to preach that when human beings were born they are naturally endowed with *de* (duh) or "virtue," and that if this built-in quality of humanity is developed there will be no need for laws and other controls on human behavior.

Lao also taught that the only legitimacy for a ruler was absolute virtue—that only a man or woman who was truly and totally virtuous could resist the corrupting influence of power and conduct the affairs of state and the people in a fair and just way.

However, Lao went on to say that there were few truly virtuous human beings in the world because the cultures created by humans did not support virtue—and Chinese history makes much of this reality.

There are numerous stories in Chinese records about rare people who were virtuous and the majority who were lacking to some degree. During the famous Ming Dynasty (1368-1644 A.D.) one high-ranking court official came up with a way of impressing the importance of virtue on government officials. He had officials who were especially notorious for enriching themselves executed. He then had their bodies stuffed and placed in their offices to remind their replacements of the fate that awaited them if they abused their positions.

Despite the rarity of truly virtuous people the Chinese still put great stock in the concept, and in all of their relationships they seek to measure the virtue of the individuals concerned. When they encounter such an individual they honor and obey him or her without question.

The Chinese concept of virtue crosses cultural lines, and therefore pertains to foreigners as well as Chinese—and the Chinese are very good at discerning and measuring the virtue of foreign businesspeople and government leaders.

China's government leaders as well as businesspeople on all levels base their relationships with their foreign counterparts on the degree of virtue they perceive in their character.

Di Sam Zhe (Dee Sahn Jay)/The Importance of Third Parties

Foreigners dealing with China should bone up on the role and importance of *di sam zhe*, or "third parties," in Chinese culture. Unlike in the United States and in most Western countries, in China the traditional way of making new contracts for whatever purpose was through third parties or go-betweens.

The reason for the use of go-betweens in China is that relationships between people were highly personalized and formal, and calling on someone without going through a third party was a serious breach of etiquette.

Throughout the millennia of Chinese history *di sam zhe* played a vital role in arranging marriages, in political alliances, and in establishing new business relationships.

Go-betweening is still a common and popular profession in China, and while the total number of marriage go-betweens is down the number of legal, business, and political consultant/go-betweens is up dramatically.

Given the intricacies of Chinese law on both a federal and provincial level, as well as the custom of using third parties to pave the way for new business relationships, foreign businesspeople who are new to China should plan on identifying and retaining go-betweens to aid them.

There are, in fact, numerous situations in China that can be resolved or moved forward only with the help of *di sam zhe*. When Chinese (and other Asians) do not have their own personal contacts or "back doors" and when conflicts occur they routinely use trusted go-betweens in their business and social relationships.

Asians will generally reveal to trusted third parties what they are really thinking—what they really want, especially when "face" is concerned. This is an approach that Westerners in China should learn and use.

Another thing to keep in mind is that generally Chinese businesspeople cannot make binding decisions on the spot. They usually have to get agreement or approval from a number of other people in their companies as well as from a number of government officials.

Another point: If you're asking for something that has not been done before, getting government agencies to set a new precedent ranges from impossible to difficult, and will definitely take time.

Again, the decision to set or not set a precedent is often not based on any law or directive. It is based on the personal choice of individual officials. They can and do make arbitrary decisions about matters that come before them.

Generally speaking their criteria is based on what is good for their department, their agency, or ministry—and often for their country.

Still another factor to keep in mind is that Chinese officials and executives generally do not delegate authority to subordinates. The implications this suggests are obvious.

Falu (Fah-luu)/Laws in their Chinese Context

One of my favorite Confucian quotes is as follows: "Attempting to rule people by laws that require them to act the same leads to resentment and disobedience of the laws and to feel no shame!"

Confucius believed that people should behave because of their inherent virtue; not because of manmade laws.

The Imperial rulers of China (as well as the present-day Communist rulers to some extent) apparently took part of this philosophy to heart because most of China's *falu* (fah-luu) or "laws" were not codified or published. It was left up to judges and others to decide on what was legal and not legal.

In present-day China there are many published *falu* but many of them retain some of the essence of Confucius by being worded vaguely—so vaguely in many cases that their purpose cannot be clearly understood. (And when most people ignore them, the government sometimes pretends they don't exist; or that they were just a test.)

Like the emperors before them, China's Communist leaders know that if the laws are vague and punishments are quick and severe most people will refrain from doing anything that might even seem to be illegal.

Still today the Communist government of China prefers to rule by directives rather than codified and published laws, which often puts foreign businesspeople and others at a disadvantage because they cannot anticipate how the directives are going to be interpreted.

The only practical approach for foreigners is to get the advice and assistance of experienced Chinese—and hope for the best.

Fuze Ren Yuan (Foo-tsuh Wren Yuu-enn)/Finding the Responsible Person

Another cultural factor that plays a vital role in China is the custom of defining the responsibilities of individuals in business and government offices down to the smallest detail.

This circumstance grew out of the extraordinary degree to which work in China was traditionally structured and specialized. There was a precise place for everything, precise equipment for doing everything, a precise way of using the equipment, and specific people of the right rank who were solely responsible for doing certain things.

This custom became so deeply embedded in the mindset of the Chinese—and it covered every mundane action in their lives, from how they held and handled chopsticks to folding clothing—that it homogenized both their way of thinking and doing things.

This degree of cultural conditioning is still conspicuous in today's China among the older generations in particular, but the upbringing of children in urban China has changed to the point that young people often do things in non-Chinese ways.

While the standardization of virtually all activity in China thousands of years ago resulted in an extraordinary degree of order and stability, it had a downside as well in that it did not permit innovation or change of any kind.

The degree of the homogenization of Chinese thinking and behavior is diminishing fairly rapidly with the internationalization of the culture but it persists to the point that in many situations one must locate the *fuze ren yuan* or "person who is responsible," before you can get something done.

If the responsible person is out of an office it is usually not possible to get anything done that he or she is officially responsible for, even though it is something very simple that could easily be handled by someone else. In some cases this can be nothing more than not being able to get permission to use a copying machine that someone else is "responsible" for.

Many of the obstacles that both foreign businesspeople and visitors alike encounter in China are caused by the absence of the responsible person.

Ganjin (Gahn-jeen)/The New "Can Do" Chinese
Until China's "get rich is glorious" era was inaugurated by Deng Xiaoping in the late 1970s most Chinese lived and worked more like bees than independent, individualistic human beings.

They were bound to their homes, their farms, shops, or factories very much like a colony of bees. Their livelihood and often their lives as well depended on them slaving away to ensure the survival of their work unit, which in turn was charged with contributing to the communist policies of the government.

Within the first decade after the beginning of the Deng era a new type of Chinese had emerged—a type that quickly became famous for their inner strength, their energy, their courage and their drive to dramatically improve their economic well-being by becoming entrepreneurs or hiring themselves out as skilled professionals.

This group of people was so culturally different from the typical Chinese that a new word, *ganjin* (gahn-jeen), was coined to describe them. The meanings subsumed in the new word included ambition, energy, strength, and the courage to take risks—the latter in particular a characteristic that had been exceedingly rare in China for centuries.

It was this new breed of people that took the lead in transforming the economy of the country and setting the stage for the cultural changes that were to create modern China.

Ganjin in present-day China now number in the millions and the number is growing with each new generation. Their motivation to succeed is incredible, and their accomplishments up to this time only begin to suggest what they will achieve in the future.

Ge (Guh)/Keeping Your Balance During Interesting Times

China's traditional culture was designed to ensure that both the government and people at large would keep their "balance" in the hierarchically structured society regardless of the provocations or pressures.

This early Chinese compulsion to ensure social and political stability was based on the knowledge that most people fear and are upset by *ge* (guh) or "change"—something that prompted China's earliest philosophers to create precise guidelines for both rulers and the ruled.

In effect, these guidelines reserved the right to make or prohibit change to the imperial government and its minions. This resulted in making common Chinese frightened of change because they had no control over things, and making those in power advocates of the status quo because they didn't want to lose their privileged positions.

China's earliest philosophers recognized that change is the only constant in the universe and they did their best to apply human control to it—an approach that was primarily manifested in the system of etiquette they devised based on the teachings of Confucius—specifically the relationships between husbands and wives, parents and children, males and females, inferiors and superiors.

At the same time, the Chinese concept of *ge* recognizes that change is essential to avoid stagnation and degeneration—something that is true of all organizations, particularly companies and governments. They also recognized that the challenge was to control change and guide it in a positive direction.

The policy of China's government since the demise of the Mao regime has been to control both economic and social change from the top down. But once the people were given enough freedom to plan and initiate changes on their own, the cat was out of the bag.

Since the 1990s change has been so pervasive and so rapid in China that it is impossible to keep up with it. The government does its best to keep the ship-of-change on an even keel but it is an impossible task. More and more it is the people of China who are steering the ship and the course is wobbly—but that is democracy in action.

Foreign businesses and governments dealing with China have to become experts in keeping up with the *ge* that are transforming the country. Almost nothing remains the same very long.

Gongwei (Goong-way-ee)/Beware the Flattery Ploy

To paraphrase an entry in my book, *China's Cultural Code Words*, there are many words in Chinese that are designed and used to show respect and deference to the elderly and superiors, to acknowledge social inferiority as well as demonstrate social superiority, to indicate sex and age differences, to account for extended-family relationships, to seek favors, etc. and etc.

This extensive vocabulary is a result of the vital importance that personal relationships have had in China since ancient times—which in turn resulted in people becoming extraordinarily sensitive to and about all of their relationships.

Another result of this situation was the role that *gongwei* (goong-way-ee), or "flattery," played in Chinese life.

With both success and survival generally depending on maintaining good relations with others—in the extreme sense—the use of flattery became a national custom that was raised to a fine art.

The use of *gongwei* is still deeply embedded in the character and personality of the Chinese, and has become one of their most valuable tools in dealing with foreigners. The Chinese learned a long time ago that Westerners—Americans in particular—are especially susceptible to flattery, and they use it with great skill in disarming and manipulating them.

Guan (Goo-een)/Contemplating Things Deeply

One of the most conspicuous traits of Americans is the desire for speed—in everything, and especially in business and particularly when they are overseas staying in an expensive hotel. The appearance of computers and the Internet were a godsend to time-conscious Americans.

This character trait often presents Americans with a variety of problems in their dealings with Chinese companies, government agencies, and the leadership of the country.

It is difficult for Americans to grasp, but the Chinese sense of time stretches across some five thousand years. Older educated Chinese in particular *feel* their history and are guided by it. They are also motivated by a powerful need to engage in lengthy *guan* (goo-een), or "contemplation," before they make important decisions.

Guan is a cultural concept that includes all of the cycles that are inherent in all life, including the cosmos—and compels wise people to take the time to understand the nature of everything that confronts them.

Most Westerners are likely to look upon this as an esoteric and metaphysical approach to the ordinary mundane things of life—like making a business deal and earning a quick profit.

But even though typical Chinese businesspeople, bureaucrats, and politicians may not consciously think in terms of *guan*, they nevertheless are culturally bound by its invisible presence to seriously contemplate their moves.

As noted in my book *China's Cultural Code Words* the goal of *guan* is to become one with the cosmic laws that control the universe, making it possible for a person to instinctively act in harmony with the cosmos.

China's ancient philosophers taught that once you understand the nature of life and yourself through contemplation you are able to exercise considerable control over business and other affairs, and what is going to happen in the future.

In any event, this sums up the thinking and goals of older Chinese because it is something they absorb from the culture.

Guanxi (Gwahn-she)/The Role of Personal Connections

From the dawn of China's ancient civilization the people were controlled by beliefs, customs, and laws that limited their ability to make personal and individual decisions. Virtually every aspect of their lives was prescribed, or was set by precedent, down to where they lived, what they wore, the work they did, the education they received, who they married, and how they interacted with other people.

Over the long millennia of Chinese history this system along with the beliefs and behavior that supported it became one of the primary foundations of the Chinese mindset. There were precise rules and ways of doing things for all social classes—rules and ways that strictly limited the rights of individuals to make personal decisions.

In such a society the old adage "It's not what you know it's who you know" becomes an axiom of life. Another truism in this kind of society is the fact that it is generally not your intelligence, knowledge, ambition, or motivation that determines your success in life. It is *guanxi* (gwahn-she), the personal connections you have and how clever you are at using them.

Guanxi is usually translated into English as "connections," but this English term does not do justice to the cultural implications and importance of the word in Chinese society. In my above mentioned book I explain the concept of *guanxi* by defining it as relationships that are based on mutual dependence.

There is, of course, a certain amount of mutual dependence in all societies but in the American mindset in particular it is generally secondary to a strong sense of individualism and independence. The American mantra is to take personal responsibility for one's actions and success or failure. Seeking and depending upon connections is not built into the American way of life.

That is not the case in China. The essence of Chinese culture, still today, is based on *guanxi*. The foreigner in China who attempts to get by without making and nurturing connections is almost always doomed to failure.

Guei Mei (Gway-ee May)/Staying Out of Trouble

The Chinese have traditionally been culturally programmed to assume and keep a very low profile in situations that might be upsetting or dangerous to their livelihood or their lives.

This element of Chinese culture was covered in the famous book *I Ching*, or *Book of Changes*, written by the legendary Chinese Emperor Fu His (2935-2838 B.C.), with additional materials added by King Wen and the famous Duke of Chou in the 11th century B.C.

The most widely read of the famed Chinese Classics (others include *The Analects of Confucius, Great Learning, Doctrine of the Mean, Mencius*, and *Daode Jing*), the *I Ching* provides an interpretation of all of the key elements in the affairs of man, using hexagrams consisting of a stack of six solid and broken lines.

Admonitions to keep a low profile to avoid repercussions, No. 54 in the *Book of Changes*, came under the heading of *guei mei* (gway may), which literally means subordinate—literally someone or something of a lower class or order that is subject to superior classes or orders.

Guei mei covers situations when the individual has little or no control over what is going on, cannot change things, and can survive only by working hard, doing nothing to call attention to himself, and patiently waiting until the circumstances change.

Traditionally the Chinese were taught to remain passive, calm, and polite; to do little or nothing to avoid making mistakes, and to do nothing more than what they were specifically supposed to do. This was especially important to the survival of millions of people during the final decade of the reign of Mao Zedong.

Guei mei cultural programming has weakened considerably in modern China but it is still visible in many ways in the character of most of the people. In companies and government agencies many people still "bury themselves" in subordinate positions or are "buried" by their superiors.

Foreign businesspeople in China quickly learn that it is necessary to literally reprogram most new employees to get them to speak up and take the initiative in their work and in their relationships with managers.

Guo Cui (Gwah T'sue-ee)/The National Essence of the Chinese

Beginning some five thousand years ago the Chinese were gradually imbued with philosophical beliefs and practical day-to-day rituals that covered every known element of human existence, infusing the people with a unique view of themselves, their surroundings, the world at large, and the cosmos.

This view, which has been labeled the *guo cui* (gwah t'sue-ee) or "national essence" of the Chinese, was to distinguish them from all other people, make their culture extraordinarily persuasive and powerful, and sustain them in the worst of times.

All of the things for which the Chinese were to become famous—from their arts and crafts to their cuisine—were products of their distinctive national essence, which was to overflow their national borders and provide the foundations of the cultures of Korea, Japan, and much of Southeast Asia.

Still today, despite the inroads made by American and other Western cultures, the national essence of the Chinese remains intact in most of the ways that count.

It has, in fact, turned out that many of the elements of China's traditional culture remain as valid and as important today as they were two or three thousand years ago—something that is gradually being realized by a growing number of people.

These people, who have their counterparts in the United States, Japan, and other industrially advanced nations, have already begun fashioning a new lifestyle that attempts to incorporate the best of the past with the best of the present.

Given the inevitability of China's continuing rise as an economic and political power it would be wise indeed for both the Chinese and other nationalities to identify those elements of China's traditional culture that are universally valid and make them an integral part of the growing international culture.

Hanyu (Hahn-yuu)/China's Secret Code Has Been Cracked

My referring to *Hanyu* (Hahn-yuu) as China's secret code is a bit of stretch that is intended to emphasize a key factor in China's historical and present-day relations with other people. *Hanyu* means "Chinese language" or "Chinese languages."

My point is that the existence of ten major Chinese languages (and dozens of minority languages and regional dialects) along with one of the most complex of all writing systems has traditionally served as the "Great Wall" of China—a wall that has helped keep the country isolated, insulated, and exclusive until modern times.

In the past so few Westerners learned Chinese that there was very little communication between ordinary Chinese and Westerners—and the bulk of that was with Chinese who had learned English or some other foreign language. As a result very few Westerners were ever able to fully understanding Chinese culture.

This failing is gradually being remedied, as more and more non-Chinese are learning Mandarin (made the national language of China by the Communist Party in 1949)—and this includes Americans, who traditionally ignored language learning as an important skill.

The famous Great Wall of China was not successful in keeping outside barbarians at bay. They not only breached the wall, they captured and ruled the country for many centuries.

Now, the wall that was far more successful in keeping most foreigners at bay in their dealings with China has been breached by a growing number of people who came not as conquerors but as friends.

Again, I am talking about *Hanyu*—which should be written as *Han yu*, the two words that it is—because it means "Chinese language," or "the language of China." There are dozens of thousands of foreigners in China today who speak good Chinese, and millions of other people around the world who have seen the future and are studying the Chinese language.

As late as the early 1990s the Chinese language continued to serve as a "secret code" for China, barring most foreigners from understanding and dealing with the Chinese in any comprehensive way. There are, in fact, ten major Chinese languages—not just one—which traditionally made the barrier of dealing with the Chinese more formidable.

However, this age-old language problem is gradually being eliminated as a result of an edict issued in 1949 by Mao Zedong, leader of the new communist government, mandating that Mandarin, the Chinese spoken in the Beijing region, would be taught in all schools throughout the vast country as the national language.

But problems continue. In Mandarin (as in the nine other sister languages of China) there is a formal language as well as a common language—and they are different enough that learning the common language does not mean that you can understand or use the formal language. It requires a new vocabulary and some new rules.

There are two vital reasons for foreigners to learn both spoken *Hanyu* and *Hanzi* (Hahn-jee), the ideograms with which the language is written, because, as noted in the Preface of this book, the culture of the Chinese, their mindset—the way they think and behave—is built into the Chinese language.

In many cases learning *Hanzi* can, in fact, be more important than learning *Hanyu*, because *Hanzi* present a visible pictorial representation of the concept expressed in the word—not just its sound and popular meaning but the origin of the concept, with its nuances.

Dissecting the *Hanzi* reveals the full context of each word, including nuances that are not obvious to anyone not raised in the traditional culture and not totally familiar with the parts that make up the ideograms.

Learning the origin of the parts of each character and how to draw them—a visual and physical as well as an intellectual exercise—imprints their nuances and uses on the student.

In other words, if you want to really understand Chinese culture in all of its depth and breadth you have to learn the *Hanzi*.

Hong (Hung)/Looking at Things Holistically

The traditional culture of China programmed the people to look at and react to things in holistic terms—that is to look beyond the surface and into the depth of things; to consider all angles, all eventualities, and to base their reactions on fundamentals rather than surface indications.

The Chinese "code word" for this cultural programming is *hong* (hung), which can be translated as "profundity"—and refers to great depth of feeling, intellect, and meaning.

This deep approach to considering things is time-consuming and often does not result in absolute, clear answers to any problem or investigation because there are factors that cannot be seen or predicted.

Westerners, on the other hand, are culturally conditioned to look at things as absolutes and often from a Christian religious viewpoint—black or white, good or bad, with little if any tolerance for variations. This viewpoint tends to gloss over things that do not fit the criteria and results in a one-dimensional view of the world.

This results in Americans and other Westerners having two moralities—one that is private and one that is public, and the two are often diametrically opposed to each other.

Not surprisingly, this difference in the way the Chinese and Westerners view the world results in misunderstandings and confrontations, and even though they may ultimate agree to cooperate with each other it is generally for the sake of expediency rather than complete agreement.

It is not always fair or valid for Westerners to expect the Chinese to compromise their beliefs and practices, so it is important for Westerners to anticipate the reactions of their Chinese counterparts, to have ready answers and to be prepared to adjust their own expectations when the Chinese side has merit.

In any event, Western businesspeople and diplomats dealing with China should be prepared in advance to have more *hong* in their proposals than they may be used to.

Hou Men (Hoe-uu Mane)/The Famous Back Door

In a society in which personal connections play a paramount role in all relationships—business, personal, political, and otherwise—the typical Western way of doing things is often ineffective, and may be considered both arrogant and rude.

In China where historically ordinary people had no inalienable rights to protect them from those in power and where bureaucracy was universal and honed to perfection, expecting something simply because it was "right" and you should get it, and especially "demanding" something or some action, would get the door slammed in your face—or far more serious results.

This situation resulted in the Chinese having to develop a variety of strategies and tactics to get things done—ways that were unofficial but were a key part of the system—like authorities allowing a black market to function because it provided them with advantages of one kind or another.

The most common of these unofficial tactics was using the *hou men* (hoe-uu mane) or "back door"—that is, contacting and making deals with people behind-the-scenes; in private.

Despite political reforms and cultural changes that have made life in China far more rational and practical, the use of *hou men* remains deeply embedded in the culture, and when there is a "back door" most people choose to take it—and if there isn't one they will generally attempt to make one.

This is usually one of the first lessons learned by foreigners working in China.

Jiaoliu (Jee-ah-oh-lew)/The Role of Mystery in Communicating

One of the dichotomies in Chinese culture that invariably conflicts with Western attitudes and behavior is in communicating—that is, the basic, fundamental act of communicating personally as well as publicly.

It has been said that there is no true *jiaoliu* (jee-ah-oh-lew) or "communication" in China. Of course there is but there are two distinct types of communication, one of which Westerners find irrational and frustrating.

The traditional type of *jiaoliu* is to speak and/or write in vague terms that may be virtually meaningless on the surface and have to be passed through a kind of culture decoding process before they can be understood. The other type of communication is precise and clear.

The reason for the vague approach to communicating was traditionally the importance of avoiding any kind of friction, resistance or embarrassment in all relationships—a factor that is still of vital importance in all relationships in China.

Another traditional aspect of *jiaoliu* in the business and political areas was the idea that the higher the executive, manager, or official the more distant and aloof they should be, and the less they should communicate with underlings about either their feelings or factual matters.

The more distant and publicly silent these individuals the more "mysterious" their image, and the more powerful they were—or could be—in the minds of people below them. Historically, the Chinese were conditioned to believe that "mystery" was the ideal qualification for a leader.

The flip side of this factor was that the people were expected to know what such mysterious figures wanted them to do without being told. Of course, this required a deep and broad knowledge of the culture—something that generally was not the case with foreigners.

The other type of communication in China is the one that Westerners are familiar with—based on terms that are as clear and as precise as possible. But this type of communication is still relatively rare in China, and is one of the cultural elements that foreigners must deal with.

The Chinese are acutely aware of the vagueness factor in their communication of whatever kind on whatever level, and on both a business and political level they take advantage of it in a variety of ways, especially where foreigners are concerned. The only recourse for foreigners who cannot decipher what they are told is to persist in round-about dialogue until the meaning or intent of the Chinese becomes clear.

Jiaoshu Yuren (Jeeow-shuu Yuu-wren)/The Chinese Approach to Learning

Before Mao Zedong unleashed his "cultural revolution" in 1966 the relationship between teachers and students in China was exceptionally close. In many respects teachers acted like surrogate parents to their students, and students in turn obeyed and honored their teachers.

For close to three thousand years teachers were among the most esteemed members of society and played major roles in the development, survival, and spread of Chinese civilization.

Teachers were seen as not only conduits for spreading knowledge among the elite of China, they were also the repository and the transmitter of the morality and guidelines necessary for the harmonious functioning of society.

This gave birth to the commonly used expression, *jiaoshu yuren*, which translates as "teaching book and teaching people how to live."

Mao Zedong did his best to completely destroy the country's traditional education system, seeing it as an unacceptable threat to the ideology and goals of communism. Before his death in 1976 he succeeded in his goal, leaving one generation without books, without teachers, and without schools.

Soon after Mao's death the new government leaders initiated efforts to rebuild the educational system, and by the beginning of the 21st century it had been restored to a considerable degree.

But by that time the culture of young Chinese had changed so fundamentally that most of them were no longer willing to totally subordinate themselves to their teachers and professors. They had grown up in personal freedom and become individualistic in their values and attitudes.

Present-day Chinese students are no longer in awe of their teachers but on the average they are far more diligent and more determined to get the best possible education than their American and other Western counterparts.

If the United States and other Western countries are not to be completely bypassed by China in the future I believe it is absolutely imperative that they take not just a page but a book from the history of China and change their education systems to one that attracts the best teachers and inspires students to do their best.

Kaolu Kaolu (Kow-luu Kow-luu)/A Discreet Way of Saying No

This expression, which means "I'm looking onto it" or "We're looking into it," is one of the most commonly used stalls in the Chinese language.

It is especially used by government officials when they cannot approve of something but don't want to come right out and say it, as well as when they want to delay the action for some reason—generally to wring concessions of some kind out of the deal.

There are occasions, however, when this reaction is not a stall. Government regulations are typically written in such a way that they can be interpreted in a number of different ways, so there are times when officials must, in fact, take time to figure out if they apply or not.

This element arises because of the fact that both the ethics and the policies of the government tend to be situational—depending on the circumstances rather than on an explicit principle—a cultural factor that was traditionally used to help maintain surface harmony by making decisions based on personal considerations.

When foreigners encounter the *kaolu kaolu* syndrome their best bet is to look for the personal factor in the situation, and if they discover it see if they can come up with an acceptable solution.

There are often occasions, however, especially on a mundane level, when a *kaolu kaolu* response simply means that the individual doesn't want to be bothered.

Liangshou Zhunbei (Lee-ing-show Juhn-bay)/Two-Handed Preparation

This expression refers to the practice of Chinese who are engaged in business negotiations with a potential new partner to be negotiating with a second party at the same time.

This "two-handed" approach is used not only as a backup but also to bring pressure on one or both of the two potential partners to gain concessions and get a better deal. This approach has been especially successful in dealing with Western companies because of the handicaps they must deal with—the language, the culture, government regulations, and their rush to get a contract signed as quickly as possible.

There is no quick, direct solution to this problem, leaving the foreign side with only one option—to play the same game, and let the Chinese side know that you have other suitors waiting in line and will go to them if the negotiations are not resolved in an equitable agreement within a reasonable length of time.

When you take this position the Chinese side will, of course, be very interested in who your other prospects are and will attempt to find out. It doesn't pay to try to bluff them because they have ways of finding out the truth.

And it is not wise to willingly reveal the identities of other prospects whether or not you are in contact with them, so the situation becomes a contest to see who will blink first. The best recourse in this kind of standoff is to bring in a mutually known trusted third party to bolster your position, especially emphasizing the advantages that would accrue to the Chinese side if they accept your terms.

Lunlixue (Loon-lee-shway)/Policies Instead of Ethics

Westerns tend to base their concept of right and wrong on principles that are absolutes. The Chinese have traditionally based their concept of right and wrong on personal considerations of the circumstances at hand, with judges, officials, and other individuals having substantial leeway in the decisions they made.

Instead of being based on a combination of logic and god-based beliefs, Chinese ethics have traditionally been based on preserving harmony as dictated by Confucianism—a harmony designed to maintain stability among and between the hierarchical classes that made up Chinese society.

Obviously this was profoundly different from the ethics that evolved in the Western world and invariably complicated encounters between Chinese and Westerners.

Most present-day Chinese still, in fact, prefer situational ethics and morality to a morality based on absolute principles because this Western approach often discounts both human feelings and what is actually best for people.

Cultural, economic, and political changes in China since the last decades of the 20th century have all combined to reduce the role of situational ethics in China, but they still exist in government, in business and in private life and they continue to have an impact on all affairs in the country.

Foreign businesspeople engaged in China must invariably take situational ethics into account in their dealings with the government, with their Chinese employees, and with their Chinese business contacts.

Luoji (Luu-oh-jee)/How the Chinese View the World

There has traditionally been a fundamental difference in the way the Chinese think and behave and the attitudes and behavior of Americans and West Europeans—a difference that is reflected in the Chinese and English terms for logic.

The Chinese term for logic, *luoji* (luu-oh-jee), means one thing and the Western term logic means something else.

Broadly speaking, *luoji* takes into consideration all kinds of diversity and contradictions. Western logic does not. It is fact-based: two times two equals four, and so on, and is primarily based on empirical knowledge based on observations and experiments.

The Chinese are perfectly capable of rational, logical thinking, as their long history of extraordinary scientific and technological achievements clearly attest, but in their human relationships they have traditionally used another standard.

It generally works very well to apply the expression "fuzzy logic" to the everyday *luoji* of the Chinese; the kind of logic—basically new to the Western world—that attempts to account for everything, not just the obvious.

The Chinese goal is to accept all things and then attempt to reconcile them in a unified whole.

Westerners try to understand and pin everything down to the lowest level; the Chinese are content to leave things flexible. In short, Chinese *luoji* gives precedence to the vagaries of humanity, and the Chinese tend to view Western logic as too cold, too anti-human.

Foreigners who attempt to deal with the Chinese on a strictly Western style logical basis, especially on a government level, often encounter a response or resistance that seems to have no logical explanation. ·

The point that Westerners should keep in mind is that the Chinese typically consider all things from a personal viewpoint, which may or may not appear rational when viewed logically.

Mei You Ban Fa (May-ee Yoh-ou Bahn Fah)/It's Not Going to Happen!

This Chinese expression has several applications, all of which are designed to give the individuals concerned an advantage in whatever talks they are involved in. The literal meaning of the expression translates into colloquial English as "no way"—meaning that the proposal or whatever is not going to happen.

Mei you ban fa is commonly used in business negotiations with foreigners, and is one of the many hardball tactics in the Chinese arsenal of negotiating ploys—tactics that often surprise and sometimes shock foreigners who have been led to believe that the Chinese are always polite in their treatment of foreign guests.

All of the initial expressions of hospitality and formal protocol that are characteristic of Chinese businesspeople and officials notwithstanding, they are tough negotiators who do their homework and play rough.

They typically demand a variety of concessions from foreign negotiators, particularly in the case of rights to technology—a position that the government strongly endorses and often refuses to approve of arrangements that do not give the Chinese side access to the technology concerned.

One of the more common uses of the *mei you ban fa* ploy is a claim by the Chinese negotiators that the government will not approve of a contract as presented by the foreign side, and that changes must be made to conform to government regulations.

Negotiators may also use the ploy by announcing that the discussions are not making any progress and that they are going to stop for a while or break them off completely.

There is no single way to counter a *mei you ban fa* announcement. The best thing the foreign side can do is to remain calm and focused, and seek to overcome the stalling tactic by approaching it from different angles.

This may involve having a third party make discreet inquiries at a government agency to see if there are, in fact, any regulations that would prevent the necessary license from being issued. This should definitely be discreet in order not to cause anyone to lose face.

Mianzi (Me-inn-jee)/Face Comes First

Another cultural factor that often plays the most significant role in both social and business relationships in China is subsumed in the word *mianzi* (me-inn-jee), which may be translated as "face" or "personal honor." The Chinese concept of "face" is broken down into four basic categories:

One that refers to the good reputation that one gets by avoiding mistakes and making what turns out to be wise decisions.

One that covers all of the actions one takes to "give face" to others by showing them respect and paying them compliments.

One that refers to others giving *you* face by treating you respectfully and saying complimentary things about you.

And finally, the "face" that refers to having actions or events that are embarrassing or damaging to you become known to other people—in this case referring to loss of face.

Given the extraordinary importance of reputation in China it is imperative that this cultural factor be understood and dealt with properly.

Mei You (May-ee Yoe-uu)/There isn't any of That!

This phrase literally means "not have" and has been described as the "great saying" of China—meaning that traditionally it has been one of the most commonly used expressions in life. It has also been compared to the Great Wall of China, since it was used in such a way that it was a barrier to getting things done.

By extension, *mei you* can mean such things as there aren't any, I don't have that, we're sold out, it's time for lunch so I can't help you, it's closing time so I can't help you, etc. In other words, it was and still is used to avoid having to do something.

When a number of shoppers with several packages attempt to board a taxi the driver may turn them down with a *mei you*. When a customer asks for something in a store that is not visible on a counter or in a showcase, a clerk who doesn't want to go to the stockroom and look for it may respond with a *mei you*.

In the past foreign visitors to China's large cities often encountered the *mei you* barrier because the individuals they confronted didn't speak English or any other foreign language and resented the loud and overbearing ways of the foreigners.

While the usage of *mei you* has diminished considerably in modern China it is still a common expression used in indirect approaches that are meant to be non-threatening and to make it easier for someone to say no or decline to do something. In this case, it is something like saying, "I don't suppose you have ... (something or other).

If you are met with a *mei you* it sometimes works to phrase your request or question in a very humble way: "I am really sorry to bother you, but...;" "Could you be so kind as to...?"

Qing (Cheeng)/Being Clear About Things

This term means "clear, lucid, and pure," and is usually translated as "clarity." In earlier times *qing* referred to both the character of people as well as that of the imperial government—and was something that philosophers taught as the ideal but was seldom if ever achieved.

In fact, the kind of clarity inferred by this term did not become possible in China until well after the end of the Mao Zedong era in 1976, because only then were the Chinese partially freed to express their thoughts in clear, lucid terms. The government of modern China is "purer" now than ever before but it is far from being as open as the ancient philosophers preached.

In today's China the term *qing* is used in such expressions as *qing bui* (cheeng bway), meaning a "clear conscience," and *qing chu* (cheeng chuu), meaning "clearly understood."

Foreigners in China can get a lot of mileage out of letting their Chinese friends and associates know that they are aware of this concept and are in full agreement with the ancient philosophers.

Qingke - Yanjiu Yanjiu (Cheen-kuh - Yahn-jew Yahn-jew)/ Wining and Dining Your Way to Success

Sharing food and drinks with family members, friends, and business associates is, of course, one of the most common of all customs, but the role that the custom plays in China is far more important than it is in most countries.

The intensely personal level of all relationships in China, combined with the vital importance of constantly renewing and strengthening these relationships, has resulted in what I call the Chinese way of "wining and dining to win"—which applies to business and personal relationships, as well as relationships with government officials.

This custom is so deeply imbedded in the culture of China that people on all levels of society typically go all out in showering guests and others with food and drink—and this includes very poor people as well.

The custom had already become so entrenched in Chinese life more than two thousand years ago that such demonstrations of hospitality became a part of the national character of the people—and not following the custom was seen as a failure to uphold the honor of China.

In business and government circles, one of the key Chinese words that applies to this custom is *qingke* (cheeng-kuh), which by itself means "invitation," or "invite a guest," and has the meaning of "wining and dining."

The Chinese learned ages ago that one of the fastest and best ways to make friends and influence people was to treat them to a sumptuous meal combined with a lot of drinking, and they continue to use it with great success, especially when foreigners are involved.

A key expression that is often used in conjunction with *qingke* is *yanjiu* (yen-jew), which can mean either "cigarettes and wine," or "research discussions."

This use of *yanjiu* came about because in earlier times when businesspeople and others invited government officials out for a night on the town they would repeat the word in a humorous manner—*yanjiu yanjiu*—so that the officials would understand that in addition to a banquet style meal they would be given cigarettes and wine to take home with them.

One may not hear *yanjiu yanjiu* anymore (the government has cracked down on conspicuous gift-giving to officials), but the custom of showering guests, business associates, and officials with extraordinary hospitality continues in full force. Government officials on the highest level are, of course, internationally known for their state banquets.

Foreigners can take full advantage of this cultural approach to all relationships in China because it naturally works both ways.

Shangding (shahng-deeng)/Keep on Negotiating

One of the most common complaints that Westerners have about their relationships with the Chinese (and other Asians) is that they never stop *shangding* or negotiating.

Westerners typically complain that even after contracts are signed the Chinese generally continue asking questions, asking for more information, and requesting changes in the agreement.

Given the state dynamics of business in China this should be understandable. Many company owners and managers in China are new to the business world. Both they and their companies are often young and they have had little or no education or experience in running a business.

They therefore tend to do what is natural for them—that is, they run their businesses in part or wholly on the basis of Chinese culture—in the manner in which they conduct all of their affairs. This manner includes all of the basic cultural elements that define and control their personal relationships.

The obvious recourse is for the Western side to be prepared for ongoing dialogue with their Chinese counterparts and to regard their questions and requests as a normal part of doing business with them.

This means keeping the lines of communication open at all times, monitoring all activities, solving problems as they occur, and making adjustments in the relationship as they needed.

This also means that the Western side should assign people to the task who can function in this environment—and who have direct access to top management in their home offices.

Americans in particular are advised to ask their own questions and keep on asking them, and to be good listeners—a characteristic and an attribute for which they are not noted.

Shehui Dengji (Shuu-whay Dung-jee)/Social Status Still Counts
Given China's long history as a country divided by social class it is not surprising that *shehui dengji* or social status still counts.

Status is provided by the historical lineage of one's name, by the schools one attended, by place of employment, rank, seniority, and still by the traditional cultural importance attached to age.

Culturally speaking, the Chinese generally do not regard a person as fully mature until they reach their forties—and age is closely associated with social status.

One of the more common mistakes that foreigners make in their approach to China is sending someone there to represent them who is not old enough by Chinese standards and does not have enough other qualifications to meet the expectations of the people they have to deal with.

It is important for foreign companies to make an effort to match the social and business status of the company executives and government officials they must interface with.

American companies are often not tuned into to this factor in their relations with China because social class is virtually irrelevant in the United States and it simply doesn't occur to them.

Fortunately, Americans and other Westerners are given considerably leeway in their interactions with businesspeople, particularly when sophisticated technology is concerned.

The higher and more important government officials the more likely they are to be in their 50s and above, and the more apt they are to take a condescending view of people who are younger than them, especially if they are still in their twenties and thirties.

Sheng (Shung)/Impressing Your Chinese Contacts

In the West the list of noted historical figures is generally heavy with military men—who often became political leaders, and sometimes statesmen, after their success in war.

In China, on the other hand, the most important historical figures are generally *sheng* (shung) or "sages," with the great Confucius (original name, Kung Chiu, also known as Kung Fu-Tse) leading most lists.

Unlike other ancient leaders in the West and Near East, military or otherwise, the Chinese were not obsessed with empire building and did not engage in wars of aggression against their neighbors. The Chinese looked inward rather than outward, and prized intellectual accomplishments and refined behavior more than they did physical prowess and aggressive action.

Instead of being driven to convert the rest of the world to their religious beliefs or to expand their borders, the Chinese culture emphasized self-discipline and harmony on a cosmic level. They were conditioned to protect and preserve their own system and to ignore everybody else.

Broadly speaking, the Chinese made knowledge and wisdom the foundation of their culture and their society, resulting in wise men being revered rather than military leaders.

This is one of the reasons why traditionally the Chinese considered their culture superior to others—a point of view that is hard to dispute. Foreign visitors and residents alike can win friends and influence people in China by demonstrating some awareness of this important element in Chinese history.

Knowing the names of several of the most revered sages of the past is a good beginning. In addition to the internationally famous

Confucius (551–479 B.C.), other names it helps to know include King Wen (?–1066 B.C.); his son, the Duke of Chou (?–1094 B.C.); Lao Tzu (604–550 B.C.); Tzu Chung (399–320 B.C.); Mencius (371–289 B.C.); and Mo Tzu (479–438 B.C.).

Another thing in the favor of the Chinese is that they have traditionally honored non-Chinese sages as well, revering all regardless of their race or ethnic origins.

The Chinese have traditionally equated age and experience with wisdom, which is one of the primary elements in their custom of respecting older people. And there is another interesting historical factor in Chinese culture. As individual Chinese aged, regardless of their position in life, they became more and more philosophical in their outlook and in their advice to younger people.

Now, an interesting change is now taking place among the younger generations of Chinese. Their heroes are likely to be business entrepreneurs who made it big and assumed the role of sages.

Shi (She)/The Power of Knowledge
The Chinese were among the first people to both recognize and institutionalize the power of knowledge. Academic and scientific endeavors were already flourishing in China by 2,000 B.C. Scientific research was pursued by large numbers of people, and academics were respected, honored, and rewarded.

Shi (she), or "knowledge," became the foundation of government, agriculture, business, laws, and social behavior. Extraordinary technological advances were made in many fields—many of which became the forerunners of some of today's most advanced technology.

Government employees were chosen on the basis of nationwide tests based primarily on philosophical texts. Despite the esoteric nature of some of these texts, the process nevertheless ensured extraordinary respect for learning and a high intellectual level of those who became government bureaucrats.

This respect for learning is still a vital element in the culture of today's China, and is playing an increasingly major role in the transformation of the country into an industrial powerhouse.

Chinese scientists and ordinary individuals have played key roles in many of the extraordinary entrepreneurial successes in the United States since the beginning of this century, and this phenomenon has just begun.

Cultural attributes that have made it possible for Overseas Chinese to survive and prosper despite tremendous barriers have now been unleashed in China. The power and potential this represents is awesome, and its impact on the rest of the world is growing exponentially.

Shun (Shune)/The "Soft Way" of the Chinese

The Chinese learned a long time ago that water, wind, celestial objects such as the moon, and other things have a powerful influence on nature as well as on human behavior.

Observation taught them that over time the incremental force of these elements could alter as well as completely destroy objects that seemed to be indestructible and eternal.

They also learned early that there are many things in the affairs of people that cannot be rushed. This knowledge contributed to the development of a culture in which haste of virtually any kind was seen as incompatible with the natural forces.

They referred to this element in all areas of nature and life as *shun*, which means "penetrating influence," and is a concept that has been an important element in Chinese culture since ancient times. The term also refers to having a precise and clear vision of one's goals.

This influence was at the heart of traditional Chinese etiquette as well as virtually all behavior, from work to such recreational and medicinal pursuits as the slow-moving *tai ji quan* (tie-jee-chuu-in) exercise (better known in the West by its Cantonese designation, *tai qi chuan*).

In addition to referring to "penetrating influence," *shun* also incorporates the nuance of softness and gentleness—meaning actions that are not obvious or disrupting in any way.

This concept had a fundamental impact on the Chinese mindset. In addition to being behind the idea that revenge taken subtly over a long period of time is sweeter that immediate gratification, it was also an element in how the Chinese reacted to enemies that invaded their country—gradually absorbing them over a long period of time.

Of course, patience was another of the key elements in the concept of *shun*—and the Chinese have epitomized this behavioral trait since ancient times.

One of Mao Zedong's greatest mistakes was ignoring the principle and role of *shun* in Chinese culture and attempting to bring about changes quickly—in months and years instead of decades. But in his obsessive attempt to change the Chinese way of thinking and behaving virtually overnight he inadvertently set the stage for just such changes immediately following his death.

However, the changes in Chinese culture since Mao's death were brought about by the introduction of a tidal wave of culture-free foreign technology into the country—not by a conscious effort to create a new culture.

The influence of *shun* in the Chinese mindset has not disappeared, even in the Westernized regions of the country and even though it may not be defined as such.

The Chinese government has repeatedly emphasized the point that change should take place at a slow enough pace that it does not disrupt domestic or international harmony, although its ability to control that pace has been dramatically limited by the changes already in place.

Foreign businesspeople and international diplomats inevitably encounter the residue of the *shun* mentality in their efforts to get fast reactions from their Chinese counterparts. The only answer to this problem is for them to adopt the same philosophy to whatever degree proves to be necessary.

Si; Ji (Suh; Jee)/Principles of Success

One of the key elements in understanding and dealing with the Chinese in business as well as diplomatic matters is their culturally conditioned custom of equating both of these endeavors with war.

As all students of China and a growing number of Western businessmen know, *The Art of War*, written around the 5th century B.C. by the famed Chinese military strategist Sun Tzu, is both the primer and the advanced course in how to succeed in war and in business.

There are only about ten thousand words in the small book, divided into thirteen chapters, each of which begins with a specific principle. The first chapter deals with *si* (suh), meaning knowledge; the second chapter covers *ji* (jee), or planning.

Another of the main points in the book is the importance of flexibility. Sun Tzu makes that point by equating planning and execution with water, which has no shape of its own. The point being that you should change your tactics according to the situation of the enemy.

Just as the Japanese did from the late 1950s on, the Chinese in the late 1970s began utilizing the principles of Sun Tzu in both their business and diplomatic efforts. Their planning and their execution have obviously been very successful in many areas and ways.

While Western companies have had considerable success in China since the 1980s, there have also been failures, mostly because of lack of sufficient knowledge about how business must be done in China, and often because the individuals charged with going into China did not know their own products and company policies well enough.

There is no single key to doing business successfully in China, but a firm grasp of all of the thirteen principles espoused by Sun Tzu in *The Art of War* is a very good start.

Song (Sung)/Knowing How to Avoid Conflict

Over their five thousand year history one of the most important cultural traits the Chinese developed was the custom of identifying, categorizing and listing virtually every aspect of nature and human affairs.

One of the most important of these lists of elements the Chinese calendar of things that impact on life was the one that was labeled *song* (sung), meaning "conflict."

Conflict was, in fact, number six on this list of categories, following creativity, response, overcoming difficulties in starting things, inexperience, and waiting for things to settle down.

Song refers to all of the many things, both internal and external, that create conflict in human affairs, but the most important individual source of conflict results from other people disagreeing with your point of view and competing with you in business and in other endeavors, particularly when you have no effective way of responding without raising the level of the conflict.

Past sages have taught that the first step you should take when you find yourself in this position is to simply to avoid getting involved in any conflict—in other words, run away to avoid a fight. The second step in the process is to control your pride and wait for the circumstances to change in your favor.

The sages point out that you should forget about winning— even when you are right—as long as the obstacles you face remain strong and adamant because if you insist in engaging in conflict you may bring disaster down on yourself.

Most Chinese today will still go to extremes to avoid open conflict, preferring instead to achieve their goals quietly and behind the scenes. They also believe in making compromises when facing unmovable forces and in bringing in third parties to mediate disputes and differences.

Foreigners involved with China should be aware of the concept of *song*, and be prepared to deal with it in ways that do not result in destroying the relationships they seek.

Tai (Tie)/When Harmony and Prosperity Prevail

In part, at least, China is now enjoying an astounding period of *tai* (tie)—an ancient concept that refers to periods of extraordinary peace and prosperity, and is one of the most important symbols in Chinese cosmology.

Tai also incorporates the concept of a time when communication between individuals and the world at large is totally open, and when people are receptive to new ideas and new things, in business as well as in politics.

Tai also incorporates all of the character traits that the ancient philosophers said should be the foundation of Chinese culture— respect for others, honesty, humility, modesty, diligence, perseverance, goodwill, and a strong sense of fairness.

China's ancient philosophers also warned that how long a period of *tai* lasts for individuals depends on the quality of their character and their goals and whether or not they are in harmony with themselves and with the cosmos.

Not surprisingly, the very practical sages said that if people slowed down and shored up their relationships during bad times, they could continue to prosper. They also pointed out that this is a good time to get rid of bad habits and develop new, positive ones that will contribute to your physical health as well as your spiritual wellbeing.

The Chinese have a kind of "tai antenna" that helps them discern when individuals are in or out of a *tai* period, and they make decisions accordingly. Many foreigners have learned the hard way that the good-times bad-times antenna of the Chinese is very accurate.

Tai Ji Quan (Tie Jee Chuu-inn)/The Great Fist of Health

In the 3rd century B.C. a Chinese physician wrote: "If you take care of yourself and exercise regularly, Heaven cannot make you ill. If you do not, Heaven cannot make you healthy."

By this time physical education that included swimming, soccer, boxing, high-jumping, stone-throwing and other sports were being taught in Chinese schools for both recreational and health purposes.

Tai Ji Quan (tie jee chuu-inn), the slow-motion Chinese exercise that many Westerners have seen and which literally means "Great Ultimate Fist," is believed to have originated during the Tang Dynasty, well over a thousand years ago and is now spreading around the world.

The Chinese believe—and there is both anecdotal and some scientific evidence to support the belief—that *tai ji quan* can both prevent and cure a number of serious ailments if practiced regularly over a period of time.

The efficacy of this form of exercise is based on the Chinese idea that the body is infused with a form of energy and that if "channels" carrying this energy to different parts of the body are blocked illness results.

There are several schools or versions of *tai ji quan*. One of them consists of thirteen movements—eight with the arms and five with the legs—that are designed to unblock and keep unblocked these energy channels. These movements are also said to stimulate the nerves and tone the muscles of the body.

Tai ji quan has traditionally been prescribed for headaches, digestive problems and rheumatism. In the 1970s and 1980s there were documented incidents of it also curing some far more serious ailments as cancer, but this remains controversial.

In the 1980s the Chinese government initiated a research program to scientifically record the results of *tai ji quan* on ailments and diseases in general. The results of this research resulted in an academy being established in Beijing to train people in how to perform the exercises properly, with graduates being dispatched around the country to set up *tai ji quan* schools.

Visitors to China might find an introductory course in *tai ji quan* one of the most interesting and beneficial things they can do while in the country.

Wang Ming (Wahn Meeng)/The Chinese Obsession to Achieve

As is well-known in the West there are occasionally people who are so dedicated to achieving certain goals that they become obsessed with the idea, and they succeed or, figuratively speaking, they die trying.

One of the most extraordinary things about Chinese culture is that it has traditionally produced such people in large numbers. Prior to modern times, however, the only way in which most of these people could utilize their drive for achievement was in self-improvement—particularly in manual skills.

This element in Chinese culture comes under the heading of *wang ming* (wahn meeng), which may be translated as "total dedication" or "total commitment"—and in the new China where for the first time in the history of the country people are virtually free to pursue goals beyond self-improvement, it is thriving.

In today's China vast numbers of ordinary people are so driven by the desire to achieve financial and social security that they work in a kind of frenzy. Some of them are so emotionally caught up in the challenge and the opportunity that they disregard moralistic and ethical concerns. The majority, however, are prompted by a higher level of *wang ming*.

It is that large majority of *wang ming* driven Chinese who have already transformed the country and are among the most formidable group of achievers in the world today. The impact that their ambitions, energy, and diligence are having on the world at large is still in its early stage.

Wenhua (Win-whah)/The Power of Chinese Culture

The literal meaning of this term is "patterns of thought and behavior." In other words, it means the culture of a people—which in the case of China is unique in many ways, from its extraordinary philosophical foundations to its continuity for some five thousand years.

Chinese culture has changed dramatically since 1949 when the Communist Party came to power—first because of Mao Zedong's attempts to totally eliminate the traditional culture and replace it with communist ideology, and then because of the introduction of capitalism and consumer market concepts into the country by his successor, Deng Xiaoping.

Capitalism has virtually buried the ideology of communism, and it has created a new culture that is a combination of the traditional and Western patterns of thought and behavior—with the theology of the West being conspicuously absent from this mix.

For what this means to China and to the world now, and what it portends for the future, all one has to do is look at Japan and South Korea—both small-scale clones of the traditional culture of China that have morphed into economic powerhouses as a result of their successfully combining Chinese philosophical concepts with Western capitalism.

In order to compete with China in the future, the Western world will surely have to reform its theological-based cultures by adopting and giving precedence to many of the philosophical elements of China's traditional culture—a process that is, in fact, already underway but at a slow pace that is invisible to most.

The contrast between present-day Chinese and American culture is especially sharp, and exposes trends in American patterns of thought and behavior that are alarming.

Wuwang (Wuu-wahng)/The Importance of Innocence

In the ideal Chinese world one of the primary virtues of all people would be *wuwang* or innocence—that is everyone would be innocent of all of the evil, malicious, selfish, and egotistical impulses that make most people less than perfect.

To elaborate further on this ancient Chinese concept, the ideal person would always act instinctively and spontaneously from what Chinese philosophers referred to as the natural goodness of man—a state in which one is able to harmonize his actions with the cosmic flow of life and nature.

In the traditional view of this concept the philosophers note that in times of upheaval people who are unable to act from their core of innocence will invariably make mistakes, bringing harm to themselves and possibly to others as well.

The philosophers add that living in a state of innocence can also make one vulnerable to outside influences that cannot be controlled—but that inherent in the concept is the promise that individuals who exude *wuwang* will not be deliberately harmed by others.

This philosophy has obviously not protected the Chinese from mass violence of all kinds, but in fact the vast majority of all Chinese throughout history have been good examples of *wuwang*—peaceful, thoughtful, generous, hospitable, honest, and hardworking.

One of the cultural skills of the Chinese has long been their ability to quickly recognized people who are naturally good, and to treat them accordingly. Westerners who exude *wuwang* have a special advantage in China.

Xiaoguo (She-ow-gwoh)/Paying Attention to Details

Americans and other Westerners are culturally programmed to pay careful attention to big details and less attention to small ones.

That is not the case with Chinese. Their holistic way of thinking prompts them to pay even more attention to small details than they do to the big ones, which they know will get full attention.

And when the small details are not spelled out clearly and completely they automatically interpret them the way they see fit. Problems invariably arise because what fits them often does not fit the foreign side.

Another important point is that a contract formally designates the *start* of a business relationship that will inevitably evolve with changing circumstances. Foreigners who sign contracts with Chinese (and other Asian organizations) should keep in mind that they are a beginning, not an end.

As usual, there is a special "code word" in the Chinese language that covers the Chinese concern with details. It is *xiaoguo* (she-ow-gwoh), which is translated as "conscientiousness" but figuratively means "concern with small things."

Westerners are frequently put off by the extraordinary concern for details exhibited by their Chinese associates, regarding such concern as a delaying tactic.

Xin (Sheen)/What You See May Not be What You Get

One of the barriers that has long separated the East and the West is the difference in the cultural meaning of facial expressions. Westerners are known for revealing their feelings through a variety of facial expressions; the Chinese and other Asians for concealing theirs.

This difference is, of course, a reflection of the cultures involved. Generally speaking and with some exceptions, people in Western cultures have traditionally been free to express their feelings both verbally and facially without endangering themselves.

Traditional Chinese culture, on the other hand, made it imperative that the Chinese control both their speech and their facial expressions to reveal as little as possible about what they were actually thinking. Failure to do this could have very serious consequences.

In the Chinese context of behavior maintaining a blank or neutral expression was considered good manners, and was regarded as a sign of *xin* (sheen) or "sincerity," in obeying the rules of their etiquette.

This moral requirement resulted in the Chinese characteristically smiling when they were faced with something embarrassing, sad, or otherwise disturbing—a kind of reverse reflex to mask their true feelings.

Foreigners unfamiliar with Chinese culture took this response to mean that the Chinese did not have the same feelings as Westerners, that they were callous and emotionally cold—a judgment that was, of course, patently false. And, of course, this was the source of the Western stereotype that the Chinese and other Asians were inscrutable, dishonest, devious, and evasive.

Chinese culture required the people to demonstrate their sincerity by conforming absolutely to all of the dictates of their Confucian morality—keeping a low profile, behaving in a humble manner, protecting their face as well as the face of others, avoiding confrontations no matter how minor, respecting hierarchy and age, and especially respecting authority.

Younger generations of Chinese no longer mask all of their feelings with stoic expresses when it comes to showing joy and sadness, but they still smile when embarrassed for whatever reason—which may be as simple as being asked a question, especially by a foreigner, that they cannot answer.

Generally, present-day Chinese demonstrate their *xin* by adhering to the dictates of their traditional culture without having to mask their feelings—and being free to express unrestrained joy and pleasure has given China a new face.

Xu (Shuu)/The Art of Calculated Waiting

Until modern times, the one characteristic that most distinguished the Chinese was that of patience—a trait that was embedded in their psyche by nature, by their authoritarian governments, and by the philosophers who created the framework for their morality.

The overwhelming importance of *xu* (shuu),or patience is the fifth element in the great *Book of Changes*, which dates back more than three thousand years and could be called the bible of the Chinese.

But *xu* does not mean just benign or neutral patience. It means "calculated waiting" with all that this qualification implies in the affairs of man—with emphasis on the fact that it takes precedence over all but a few of the factors controlling and impacting on human life.

China's sages made the point that exercising *xu* was the most crucial during times of chaos, particularly when political opponents were fighting each other and when immorality, corruption, and violence of whatever nature was stalking the land—and when new causes and new concepts were being introduced into the country.

The role and importance of *xu* has been especially tested in China since the end of the last imperial dynasty in 1911, particularly during the long Communist-Nationalist civil war in the 1930s and 40s and the so-called government-led Cultural Revolution from 1966 to 1976—when Chairman Mao Zedong attempted to eliminate all vestiges of Confucian and other traditional thought from the mindset of the Chinese.

Since the beginning of the post-Mao era of cultural war and repression the *xu* principle in Chinese culture has been tested by the introduction of new ideas and new processes that are continuing to remake the country.

Foreigners dealing with China should be aware of the *xu* concept, especially the element of "calculation" that is at its heart, and incorporate it in their own behavior.

Yi (Eee)/Righteousness the Chinese Way

As noted earlier, the ideograms that make up the Chinese system of writing are based on real-life things, making them very powerful in their influence on the mindset and behavior of the Chinese.

The first "building block" in the ideogram for righteousness (*yi*) is the symbol for sheep—an animal equated with well-behaved docility. The other two radicals in the ideogram are a hand and a spear—the hand representing mankind and the spear representing determination to pierce the heart of any matter concerned with righteousness.

This combination of docility, man, and the power to be righteous in all things was the foundation of the philosophy taught by Confucius and other great sages—the idea being that it was a seed that had to be continuously cultivated in order to properly influence human behavior.

Both Confucius and Mencius, his most influential follower in later times, taught that *yi* should be the basis for a universal philosophy that would allow humanity to achieve its fullest potential.

As is well known, however, this great truth did not change the ways of China's rulers and elites.

Yi has not disappeared from the culture of present-day China. In fact, there are at least five kinds of *yi* that are thriving: Communist righteousness, Socialist righteousness, capitalist righteousness, Confucian and Mencian righteousness, and the righteousness of ordinary people striving to survive and prosper in a situation where policies take precedence over principles.

These five kinds of righteousness (there are others, including those with a religious base) present an ongoing problem to both ordinary Chinese and foreigners alike. All are faced with identifying and dealing with the kind or kinds of righteousness they encounter in going about their affairs. In other words, what is regarded as right by a government official often does not conform to any of the other kinds of righteousness, and so on.

Broadly speaking, foreigners dealing with China would be better served by first taking the Confucian-Mencian approach to right and wrong—which is non-threatening—and then adjusting their behavior as far as necessary to accommodate the demands of other forms of righteousness they will inevitably encounter—without compromising their own principles and standards.

Youyi (Yohh-ee)/The Friendship Factor in China

Close personal *youyi* or friendships are essential for success in business in China. The reason for this is quite simple. The Chinese are not used to basing their business relationships on a body of laws that detail how people will conduct their business and behave toward each other. There is a growing body of such laws but they are not deeply ingrained in the cultural mindset of the people. And in any case, friendship comes first in both one-on-one and business relationships

In fact, China has a special category for people who are formally and officially referred to as "Friends of China"—a title that is reserved for people who make a career of helping China.

The importance of establishing friendly relationships with your business counterparts is an obvious reason why doing business in China is time consuming. Broadly speaking, these relationships must go beyond just being "friends" in the general sense. They must be deeper than that—deep enough that trust can be taken for granted.

The Chinese know that just signing a business contract may have little to do with how the business relationships actually develop in the future. They know that that depends on the character and personality of the people involved—and that is why they feel compelled to establish friendship ties before engaging in business with anyone.

Zhenchengde (Jun-Chuung-duh)/The Measure of Your Sincerity

This word is generally translated into English as "sincerity," but in its Chinese context it means a great deal more than it does in English. Broadly speaking, the reason for this is that Chinese culture has traditionally been far more structured, far more precise, and virtually universal in its application than the common cultures of the West.

In short, however, the reason for the extraordinary role that *zhenchengde* has traditionally—and still today—played in the lives of the Chinese is because of the vital role of personal relationships.

In feudal as well as modern-day China life still revolves around personal relationships, not only on a family level but in all public and professional activities. The Chinese spend a great deal of time, effort, and money in establishing and maintaining personal relationships because their culture has never supported individual, independent, objective thought and action.

In other words, historically in China you could not just walk in and initiate some kind of business with a person or company.

You had to first establish a personal connection. Generally speaking, the same cultural imperative applies today.

This factor makes sincerity one of the most important cultural attributes a Chinese can have, and is something they seek and must find in a person before making proposals or commitments.

The "sincerity probe" of the Chinese is always on when they meet someone new, especially foreigners because cultural differences make it difficult for them to read the *zhenchengde* of non-Chinese.

Americans are generally the most difficult for the Chinese to read because their culture is not as well-defined as most others. Unlike the Chinese who have been homogenized by millennia of the same and similar experiences, Americans tend to be mavericks in thinking and behavior.

All foreigners dealing with China should be aware of the importance of being sincere in both their speech and actions—and keeping in mind that in its Chinese context *zhenchengde* means behaving according to *Chinese* expectations.

I am not suggesting that foreigners compromise their own values and principles in order to cater to the Chinese, but that they be prepared to explain them and to insist on them when they are fair and mutually beneficial.

Another point that foreigners should keep in mind: the Chinese regard anyone who talks a lot as inherently insincere; as someone who cannot be trusted. This is another disadvantage that many Americans in particularly must somehow overcome.

Broadly speaking the Chinese believe that people who are big talkers do so in an effort to mask their lack of knowledge, experience, and understanding of human nature. In Chinese culture, the wise man speaks only when necessary.

Zhengti Guannian (Juung-tee Gwahn-nee-inn)/More About the Chinese Way of Thinking Holistically

Foreigners should be aware of and must take into account the fact that the Chinese are programmed to think holistically—that is to emphasize all of the various aspects of a matter and to consider it from the viewpoint of the interdependence of all of its parts.

On the surface, this appears to be simple common sense, but it is not simple and whether or not it is common sense depends on the culture involved. As it happens, Westerners are not specifically programmed to think in holistic terms.

Engineers are among the few Westerners who are deliberately trained to think holistically to some degree, but since such thinking is unnatural to them it is often limited to things that are relatively obvious as being essential to the performance of whatever they design and build—or that are mandated by limitations set by cost and time.

Until the modern era cost and time were not overriding factors in the thinking and behavior of the Chinese. Except for seasonal factors, they were not programmed to think in those terms. This has, of course, changed but they still today tend to view everything in more holistic terms than Westerners.

Foreigners dealing with Chinese businesspeople and government officials are prone to react to the holistic factor in their mindset by becoming impatient and frustrated. While it won't necessarily speed things up, it helps when the foreign side is aware of this cultural element in Chinese behavior.

On the plus side, it often happens that the slow, cautious, and comprehensive approach of the Chinese turns out to be the more productive than the short-term Western approach.

Zhenshi (June-she)/Dealing with Circumstantial Truth

One of the characteristics of traditional Chinese culture that Westerners found especially disturbing was the nature and role of *zhenshi* (june-she) or truth in Chinese society.

The "truth" in the usual Western sense is a statement of fact or belief that is factual as far as the speaker is concerned, with no reservations, no intention of hiding or misrepresenting anything. Of course, Westerners can and do lie outright and shade their representations of truth to suit or benefit themselves, but that does not change the definition or intent of truthful statements.

In pre-modern China, on the other hand, where there were neither laws nor customs that protected people when they told the truth, telling the truth became situational or circumstantial.

That is, it was not necessarily based on facts or factual beliefs, but on what best served the speaker.

The use of circumstantial truth was especially rampant in China during the revolutions of the 20th century, particularly during the 1966-1976 Cultural Revolution when telling the truth became a virtual death sentence, and it has not yet disappeared from the culture.

There are still situations today when individuals resort to circumstantial truth to protect themselves or to further some enterprise, as well as simply to avoid being bothered or taking on responsibility—but these instances are slowly diminishing, especially among the younger generations.

Generally speaking, the use of situational truth is the most common among government officials who can have a variety of reasons for not telling the whole truth and nothing but. These events include such rationales as stalling applications for licenses, killing applications altogether, a ploy to force applicants to change their applications, and so on.

It is often possible for foreigners as well as Chinese to detect situational truth when they hear it, but on those occasions directly confronting the teller is not a good idea. It is far better to bring in a trusted third party or to take a new polite, diplomatic tack to see if you can arrive at the real truth.

Zhongcheng (Johng-chung)/Loyalty in Today's China

The Chinese have traditionally considered loyalty one of the most desirable virtues of human beings, and it has been prescribed endlessly by the sages, by the governments, and by individuals.

But *zhongcheng,* like so many other qualities in Chinese culture, has traditionally been circumstantial and limited to specific individuals and groups of people. Chinese history is filled with extraordinary examples of individual and group loyalty, but it is also rife with examples of disloyalty on both a small and grand scale.

Within the context of China's imperial and briefly nationalist and communist governments, loyalty to those in power was literally mandatory for one's survival—and just as often as not was enforced rather than freely given. People found to be or believed to be disloyal were dismissed or exterminated.

Until the Cultural Revolution from 1966 to 1976 the one area in which there was real loyalty that survived over the generations was within nuclear and extended families. For many, that cataclysmic period destroyed even family-based loyalty, as people were forced or seduced into turning family members in to revolutionary courts.

In present-day China loyalty has returned to the fore among nuclear as well as extended families, and is one of the most stabilizing and progressive factors in society.

This does not extend across the board into the business or political world, however, as behavior in these areas has become more Western than Chinese. Companies must take extraordinary measures to attract and keep good employees. Now that job-hopping is permitted (it was illegal until the post-Mao period), it has become commonplace.

Foreign employers in China face a daunting task in becoming familiar enough with today's prevailing culture that they can deal effectively with finding and keeping worthwhile employees. The approach must be personal and it must include various considerations for the employees' families.

Zhong Fu (Chong Foo)/The Pursuit of Insight

This phrase translates as "insight" as well as "inner truth," and is one of the basic foundations of China's traditional culture. Ancient China gave birth to many philosophers who devoted their lives to seeking the truth about the nature of humanity, about nature in general, and how everything relates to the cosmos.

Some of their conclusions were wrong, but many of them were right and predated the development of such insights in the Western world by several thousand years. In fact, some of the correct conclusions reached by the Chinese more than three thousand years ago are still not fully understood or accepted in the West.

The principle of *zhong fu* begins with "know thyself" because it was recognized that you can't understand others or nature at large if you don't understand yourself.

China's ancient philosophers noted that among the requirements for achieving insight and inner truth it was necessary to be totally opened minded and have absolutely no prejudices before you can know yourself, and then you must be able to intellectually, emotionally, and spiritually merge yourself with others before you can truly know them.

Once you have accomplished this goal you are said to be in a state of *zhong fu*—and in this state you become like a magnet, attracting other people to you without effort; people who will look upon you as a leader and will do your bidding without question.

Chinese culture today still virtually compels everyone to at least attempt to achieve *zhong fu*, and the more experience they have and the older they are the closer many get to that goal. The large number of celebrated business tycoons that China has produced—past and present—owe their success and their exalted reputations to their image as paragons of *zhong fu*.

This is an emotional and personal approach to business (and other matters) that is more or less alien to the American mindset, and is one of the reasons many Americans have difficulty meshing their more objective and fact-based culture with the Chinese.

It pays for Westerners to keep in mind that the Chinese have a built-in cultural need for having a *zhong fu* type of relationship in all of their dealings.

Zhongguo Tong (Johng-gwoh Tung)/The Dangers of Being an Expert

This expression means "China Expert," and is also the equivalent of "old China hand." Being a Zhongguo tong has many advantages, but it also has some disadvantages that often put old China hands in an awkward position.

As it happens, the Chinese are very clever at using China experts to gain an advantage for themselves. This can involve a number of tactics that are usually accompanied by extreme flattery—something that most Westerners, especially Americans, are exceptionally susceptible to.

Among the most common ways the Chinese to take advantage of foreign experts is to get them to use their foreign contacts and influence to get a son or daughter a job in a foreign organization, to get them accepted by a foreign university and a visa to the country concerned, and to impress someone in a Chinese company or a government official that they want something from.

Of course, these are things that friends typically do for each other, but there is a tendency for many Chinese to carry their friendship with foreign experts to the extreme, often putting them in embarrassing positions.

The advice from other experts—those who have been used to excess by their Chinese contacts—is to diplomatically but firmly make it known that there are to limits to such favors, and restrict them to things that are reasonable for all viewpoints.

There is more to the seemingly laudatory title of China expert once you become known as one: the title, in the minds of the Chinese, automatically obligates you to "understand" the Chinese position in all matters, and this understanding includes the idea that you agree with them in whatever they say or do.

If you fail to live up to the expectations that come with the title of *Zhongguo tong*, by criticizing or not defending China, you will be regarded as a two-faced "traitor." This can be a trap for both businesspeople and diplomats—especially the latter—and is a trap that the Chinese have no compulsions about springing.

One of the ways you can defend yourself (if you really do know a lot about Chinese attitudes and behavior) is to continuously say that you are a foreigner, don't really know anything about China, and never will because China is too difficult for any foreigner to understand.

Zhongjian-Ren (johng-jee-inn-Wren)/The Very Helpful Go-Betweens

As noted earlier, go-betweens have traditionally played a vital role in Chinese life in arranging marriages, but their traditional role encompassed far more than just helping families marry off their sons and daughters. They were essential figures in both business and politics.

The role and importance of *zhongjian-ren* in China was a natural outgrowth of the limitations put on the behavior of the Chinese by Confucian and other philosophical concepts that made families the core unit of society and made relationships outside of families subject to extremely narrow and detailed rules that prevented members from freely making friends or business contacts as desired or needed.

This system included matters of protecting one's "face" as well as the faces of others, the importance of maintaining the prescribed inferior-superior codes of conduct between classes, and the extreme sensitivity of the Chinese to rebuffs and failure.

These and other elements in the traditional etiquette of the Chinese resulted in go-betweens playing significant roles in the conduct of personal, business, and government affairs.

In present-day China the importance of go-betweens in conducting business and dealing with government officials remains significant, but far less so than it was in earlier times.

Much of the role of go-betweens is now played by consultants and advisors, who can be invaluable to foreigners and foreign companies who do not have the prerequisite contacts to guide them through the political and social maze of China today.

Zou Pengyou (T'su-oh Pung-yoh-ou)/You Must Make Friends in China

This expression means making friends or to make friends—traditionally one of the most critical things in Chinese culture. In the past in China one did not just go out and meet someone coincidentally or on purpose and make friends, as is common in the West.

All relationships in China were so personally oriented and personally driven that in virtually all cases people made friends only through personal family contacts and through school and work contacts.

In the case of businesspeople needing contacts that were outside of their family, school, and company networks it was necessary to get introductions from third parties who were well acquainted with the individuals you wanted to meet and were in good standing with them.

This process did not happen quickly. It generally took weeks to months if not years, and involved a lot of time and money. Making cold calls for any purpose was virtually unthinkable. Even if a company wanted to buy something from another company a relationship had to be developed first.

The basis for relationships in the West—similar interests, similar experiences, etc.—did not apply in China.

This cultural imperative is not as strong now as it was before the beginning of the capitalist and consumer market era in China (say the 1980s), but it still plays a significant role in the conduct of business, especially when foreigners are concerned.

Western companies wanting to do business in China should formulate a clear, precise plan for getting personal introductions to the people they want and need to meet and to allow a significant amount of time to begin and develop the necessary friendships.

Trust is not an automatic element of Chinese culture. It has to be earned.

Selected Bibliograhy

Chow, Gregory (2007). *China's Economic Transformation*. Wiley.

De Mente, Boyé Lafayette (2007). *Chinese Etiquette & Ethics in Business*. McGraw-Hill.

De Mente, Boyé Lafayette (2008). *Etiquette Guide to China*. Tuttle Publishing.

De Mente, Boyé Lafayette (1996). *China's Cultural Code Words*. McGraw-Hill.

Fernandez, Juan Antonio (2006). *China CEO: Voices of Experience from 20 International Business Leaders*. Wiley.

Gries, Peter Hays (2004). *China's New Nationalism: Pride, Politics and Diplomacy*. University of California Press.

Hessler, Peter (2006). *Oracle Bones: A Journey Between China's Past and Present*. Harper-Collins.

Kynge, James (2007). *China Shakes the World: A Titan's Rise and Troubled Future*. Mariner Books.

Lovall, Julia (2006). *The Great Wall: China against the World: 1000 B.C. – 2000 A.D.* Grove Press.

Mulder, Rowin R. (2006). *China Behind the Smile*. Athena Press Publishing Co.

Tadla, Ernie (2007). *How to Live and Do Business in China*. Trafford Publishing.

Magazine and Newspaper Sources

Asian Magazine
Asia Times Online
Asia Business
Beijing Evening News
China Daily
China Today
Far East Economic Review
Financial Times
Global Times
Insight
Mainichi Daily News
People's Daily Online
People's Liberation Army
South China Morning Post
Sunday Morning Post
The Nikkei Weekly
Xinhua News Agency
Yomiuri Daily News

INDEX